The
Speed
of Light

The Speed of Light

Dialogues on Lighting Design and Technological Change

Linda Essig

Watkins College
of Art & Design

HEINEMANN
Portsmouth, NH

Heinemann
A division of Reed Elsevier Inc.
361 Hanover Street
Portsmouth, NH 03801–3912
www.heinemanndrama.com

Offices and agents throughout the world

Vari-Lite is a trademark of Vari-Lite International; Source 4 is a trademark of Electronic Theatre Controls.

Library of Congress Cataloging-in-Publication Data
Essig, Linda.
    The speed of light : dialogues on lighting design and technological change /
Linda Essig.
      p. cm.
    ISBN 0-325-00508-7 (pbk.)
    1. Stage lighting. 2. Stage lighting designers—United States—Interviews.
I. Title.
    PN2091.E4 E887 2002
    792'.025—dc21

                                             2002005923

Editor: Lisa Barnett
Production service: Sarah Weaver
Production coordinator: Lynne Reed
Cover design: Night & Day Design
Typesetter: Tom Allen
Manufacturing: Steve Bernier

Printed in the United States of America on acid-free paper
06   05   04   03   02   DA   1   2   3   4   5

For Simon and Monica, born, along with this book,
between the first interview and the last.

Contents

Acknowledgments

This is a work of recollection: my own and those of the lighting designers and industry professionals I spoke with or contacted over a five-year period. As it is an oral history, this book would not exist without the cooperation of the twenty designers, manufacturers, and engineers whose interviews make up the majority of the text you are about to read. These outstanding people are Ken Billington, Allen Branton, Dave Cunningham, F. Mitchell Dana, Jeff Davis, Bill Florac, Fred Foster, Mitch Hefter, Neil Peter Jampolis, Natasha Katz, Tom Littrell, Curt Ostermann, Dennis Parichy, Gordon Pearlman, Jane Reisman, Brad Rodriguez, Steve Terry, Bill Warfel, Marc B. Weiss, and Richard Winkler. Brief biographies of each can be found at the back of the book. I spoke with a number of other important members of the lighting community during my circuitous route through this active period in lighting history, including the late Martin Aronstein, Allen Lee Hughes, Martin Moore, Tharon Musser, Ken Vannice, and Keny Whitwright. Although they declined to be formally interviewed, their comments were helpful nonetheless. If I have inadvertently left anyone off this list, please accept my apology.

Creating a work of oral history would have been impossible without the assistance of three dedicated graduate students—now all working professionals—who provided the transcriptions of these interviews: Ellyn Kestenbaum, John Marty, and Peach Pittinger.

Students in my graduate design seminars have read a number of drafts of the manuscript in whole or in part over the years, and I thank them for their feedback on the structure of the book and for catching a number of typographical errors: John Marty, Alex Rodinsky, Maggie Bailey, Andrea Bilkey, Matt Ulrich, Dan Gallagher, Kirk Domer, Michael Cottom, and Harry Waters, Jr. Heinemann Drama's anonymous reviewers provided welcome feedback on the content and style of the book.

Part of the research for this book was funded by a grant from the UW–Madison Graduate School Research Committee.

My editor at Heinemann Drama, Lisa Barnett, provided support and encouragement during the final stages of the writing. Her support and encouragement were surpassed only by that of my dear husband, Ethan Aberg, who read the manuscript more times than he would care to admit.

Introduction

Delayed by a musician's strike, an intimate musical that had begun its life in a not-for-profit theatre in Greenwich Village opened on Broadway in October of 1975. This production, *A Chorus Line*, was unique in many ways: its nonnarrative structure, its self-reflexive qualities, its minimal setting—all of which led to the need for an unusually, for its time, specific and clearly articulated lighting environment. It was a production that I saw on Broadway at least a half dozen times during its thirteen-year run and one that I credit (or blame) for my interest in theatre and lighting design. The lighting design by Tharon Musser, highly publicized for being the first on Broadway to employ a computerized lighting control console, made the mosaic structure of that production possible.

Twenty years later, the completion of my first book gave me cause to pause and reflect on both the evolutionary and revolutionary changes that have occurred in lighting design art and technology since I first became interested in those fields. On a trip to New York in June of 1995, I saw a production that caused me not just to casually reflect but also to actively examine some of the changes that have occurred. The production that struck this chord was not a megamusical blockbuster but a one-woman show at New York Theatre Workshop (now well-known and well-financed by its production of *Rent*). *Prisoner of Love* was a nonnarrative adaptation of Jean Genet's autobiographical last book, a memoir of his time spent in the Mideast. In her design of the lighting, Frances Aronson employed—in addition to a very modest number of conventional ellipsoidal reflector spotlights, fresnels, and PAR cans—a single "Intellabeam" moving mirror fixture to catch the face of Ruth

Maleczech as if in freeze frames, seemingly to punctuate internal monologues. I did not buy a ticket to the production with the intention of seeing an unusual application of an automated light, but rather to see the work of Maleczech and JoAnne Akalaitis, the director and coadaptor. Yet sitting in this very small house, not known in its pre-*Rent* days for lavish production budgets, I was seeing the integration of automated and conventional lights in a way that a few years earlier would not have even been conceivable.

On this same trip, I visited a colleague, Allen Lee Hughes, who had a new musical in previews at The Theatre at St. Peter's Church. Looking up at the lights (or really across at them, since the back of the house puts you just a few feet below the very low grid), I noticed half a dozen or so of Vari-Lite's VL5 fixtures, which had just recently been introduced to the market. Vari-Lite was marketing these fixtures for use in the "legitimate" theatre because they had no noise-producing fans and could run on conventional dimmers. Vari-Lite had apparently loaned the fixtures to the production so that Hughes could try them out. This was the first time he had used automated lights in any significant way, and the integration of the fixtures with the conventional lights on a single console was working "less than seamlessly."

What has made such integration, however flawed, possible? Or even desirable? How has computerized control affected the American theatre? How has automation altered director, designer, and audience expectations? What do the people who work with all of this new technology really think of the technological developments of the past twenty years? Rather than try to answer these questions in a vacuum, I decided to interview people—the people who drove the technological change, the people who were affected by it, the people who exploited it for artistic effect and commercial gain.

Lighting design for the American theatre has changed fundamentally over the past twenty years. As recently as the 1950s and 1960s it was common practice for a set designer or director to merely tell an electrician which lights (colored in stock combinations of pink/blue or lavender/amber) to turn on and when. In the year 2000, it is unlikely that a set designer or director would even know how to ask for a specific light. This is not because the set designers and directors are not as well informed as in the past, but rather that lighting technology has rapidly become so complex that it requires a specialist not only to design the look of the lighting, but also to execute it. Along with this increased complexity and need for specialization has come freedom—the freedom for playwrights, directors, and designers to conceive of productions where no technical limitation is too great (budgetary constraints notwithstanding).

The specificity of lighting control and subsequent integration of the control of fixed-focus lights and automated (moving) lights was obviously made possible by computerized lighting control. The prevalence of automation was caused in part by the popularity of Vari-Lites in the concert industry. In addition, the integration of automated lights with more conventional lights for theatrical use was made possible by the standardization of control protocols, enabling many other manufacturers to enter the moving light industry. Thus, my research and interview questions revolved around three events: the introduction of the computer console to commercial theatre in 1975 on *A Chorus Line*, the introduction of the Vari-Lite on the 1980 Genesis tour and subsequent prevalence of automated lighting, and the adoption of the DMX512 control protocol which, although not originally its intent, made automated lights and peripherals accessible to the theatrical user. Along the way, people recollected their first experiences with computer light boards, the ways in which their own design process has—or in most cases has not—changed, the effect of new technology on the aesthetic of theatre, and even the changing intellectual property environment within which new products are developed. And many of them tell a darned good story![1] What follows, then, is not an actual dialogue, but a virtual one: lighting professionals talking about issues of importance not only to other lighting professionals but to anyone watching the stage.

---

1. The interviews have been edited for clarity and intermixed with one another for narrative effect.

SECTION 1

The Advent of Computer Control in Commercial Theatre

The year 1975 is immortalized forever in lighting history as the year in which *A Chorus Line* opened on Broadway, the first production to do so with a memory (i.e., computerized) lighting control console. Computer control consoles and microprocessor technologies developed later provided the foundation upon which future advancements in lighting technology were made. Our story of developing technology therefore begins with the introduction of the LS-8 console in 1975. Or does it? Lighting designer Ken Billington and others responded.

<u>KEN BILLINGTON:</u> I remember memory-controlled lighting for many years before the mid '70s. Are we just talking about Broadway or do you want me to talk about the world?

<u>LE:</u> *The world.*

<u>BILLINGTON:</u> Memory control existed all over the place. Peggy Clark was using memory boards in 1960 for the Los Angeles Civic Light Opera. This was the one that had been developed by George Van Buren on the West Coast. He developed one of the first memory consoles. . . . I remember when I was at Lester Polakov's studio in 1964 taking lighting classes with Peggy, she used to go off and light musicals for Los Angeles Civic Light Opera every year on a memory console.

Memory control was great, but it was not being embraced because it was scary.

<u>LE:</u> *What made it scary?*

BILLINGTON: What made it scary was the unknown. It wasn't scary for me because I've always been one of those people who has said, "Hey, all this can do is make our life better."

LE: *It's interesting to hear about what happened before 1975, because clearly computers were in other parts of the country before they were on Broadway . . .*

CURT OSTERMANN: My first experience with computer control was on a Van Buren board at the University of Michigan. When I came across that Van Buren board it was 1970. I graduated from high school in '70 and went right into college, so it was '70 to '74 at Michigan. They had just built a new theatre called the Power Center for the Performing Arts, which was a Jo Mielziner design based on the same design as the Beaumont in New York, except that the interior was white cement instead of black cement. We had a Van Buren board there. I was told at the time it was the first computer board in the United States, but I'm not sure that's true. I worked with that board for four years. Van Buren supposedly was involved with the Light Palette design, but this is way before the Light Palette.[1]

BILLINGTON: So, this wasn't new in the mid '70s. In the '70s it was new on Broadway, but Peggy Clark was using them long before that. I remember being in London in '68 as an assistant designer on a show and going over to Thorn Lighting and looking at the Thorn Q-Level, I think it was called, looking at memory boards there. And then in the late '60s, I remember going to the Ottawa Performing Arts Center—I don't know what show I was doing—but there was a C-Core memory by Strand. These were truly fundamental. They would cross fade from cue 1 to cue 2 and you would probably have to enter in the time of each cue or it was a manual cross fade. . . . They were very rudimentary except that they remembered. There was no such thing as a monitor screen.

LE: *Yes, that came later, I believe on Skirpan's Auto-Cue system.*

BILLINGTON: There were ways to see read-outs and they were all a little

---

1. The Strand Light Palette was developed by Dave Cunningham, who had worked for George Van Buren before moving on to Strand Lighting. It was the most popular control console on Broadway throughout the 1980s and into the 1990s.

different on each console and there were lots of numbers. And it was very interesting.

MARC B. WEISS: My first experience with memory control was with George Izenour's physical card memory board in 1966–67 at the Loretto Hilton Center at Webster College in St. Louis where I was there as the first ever TD [technical director] and hired on in part to act as the liaison and the theatre's representative in dealing with the contractors and installers of the system. But my first computer memory experience as a lighting designer was probably around 1974 on the Q-Level by Kliegl. I liked it because on the left were two columns of buttons from 0 to 9 and next to it a rate wheel. What made it great is that you could punch in any combination of two numbers to access the presets from 0 to 99. It was a way to combine the best of preset with memory.

JANE REISMAN: Oh, yes, computers were everywhere; every theatre I went out to usually, by '72 . . . and there certainly were a lot of preset boards around.[2]

BILLINGTON: At that time, the legitimate Broadway theatre had never gone past piano boards.[3] They went from piano boards to memory consoles. They skipped the preset board. While the regional theatres and the world of schools and all that went to presets—because somebody had invented them, not that they were good or bad—but they existed.

NEIL PETER JAMPOLIS: Way back when I was in school at The Goodman, we had an Izenour ten-scene preset board which—like all preset boards—was a nightmare. Now I refuse to have presets anywhere around. In teaching and all of that, the thinking is just too strange on them. But I started lighting with one of those pretty early. And . . . then when I was working as an assistant at Lincoln Center in the late '60s, they had one of the card reader systems during the John Gleason/David

2. Preset boards are an early type of electronic—but still manual—control system in which cues are set up on banks of sliders. Master sliders were used to "cross fade" from one bank to another.
3. "Piano boards," also known as "road boards," were packs of resistance dimmers—large, ungainly mechanical devices.

Hays[4] period there. It was very helpful, except that it was extremely flaky, and the cards would get jammed up, and every time that you changed a cue after the show was written, you had to redo all the cards. I thought it was really much more trouble than it was worth.

OSTERMANN: I remember that the Van Buren console [at University of Michigan] was the only one of its kind. It did not have a removable disk. So it was volatile memory in there, and there was no way to record to disk. The show was there or it wasn't, and you never knew until you pressed the Go button. Because it was a new installation we figured out problems as we went along. I did a show in September of the year it was installed, so it was one of the first shows on it, and it started losing cues (we had a lot of problems). It turned out that that was the first time we figured out that heat was a huge problem with those boards. Any time the room got over 75 degrees, the computer would no longer remember anything. Or it would be remembering cues incorrectly, which was even worse. So we installed air conditioning in there so it was 65 degrees or even 60 degrees all the time, and it was freezing. Then we discovered another problem—the booth was carpeted. It was one of the first times we came across static electricity being a problem, so we took the carpeting out.[5] Since the board didn't have a removable disk it was really inconvenient, but nobody realized it at the time.

LE: *Did you have someone from Van Buren who worked with you on solving these problems?*

OSTERMANN: No, our main lighting technician was on the phone with Van Buren constantly. And Van Buren basically fixed it with him every day on the telephone. Or exchanged cards, or told him how to solder new things on the card, and so on.

LE: *I actually had never heard of Van Buren as a company name until I walked into the Power Center in 1996 while I was designing an opera for*

---

4. Gleason and Hays were resident designers at the Vivian Beaumont Theatre at Lincoln Center throughout the 1960s and '70s.
5. The small voltage surge from a spark of static electricity could cause the core memory of some of these early consoles to be wiped out.

University of Michigan in one of their other spaces, and the Power Center had 57 dimmers. I thought, why 57, why not 60, why not 52?

STEVE TERRY: They were Van Buren dimmers, right?…Van Buren was bought out by a company called Siltron Illumination, which basically did fluorescent ballasts and emergency lighting systems. They were totally outside this industry. And they produced a line of dimmers called the Van Buren Signature Series dimmers by Siltron Illumination. As a matter of fact, Production Arts ended up buying a lot of those. They were the foundation of our touring racks of the early 1980s. We then began manufacturing that product under license from Siltron, that dimmer. So there's kind of a long connection there . . .

Memo-Q. That was another Van Buren system under the Strand name. It went into the New Orleans Theater for the Performing Arts; that would have been around '73, something like that. I think that was a pretty big development by Van Buren. Van Buren must have been working for Strand, but I'm hazy about the connection between those two.

BILLINGTON: Electronic dimmers existed, but presets on Broadway were unknown and nobody wanted to spend that money because we didn't have electronic dimmers on Broadway. A little footnote in history going back before that is all theatres in America were direct current in the 1950s. I think the basic reason we did not have electronic dimmers on Broadway was because 90 percent of the theatres were direct current. They weren't AC at all.[6] Back in the old days, [the rental shops] didn't want to spend much money on anything. For Broadway shows, they will go out and get anything now. There was a time there when they didn't have very many 6 X 16's, so you had to pick your 6 X 16's carefully.[7] A 6 X 16 was a strange new light. In the '60s, even in the late '70s, a 6 X 22 was unusual. I remember ordering twenty-four of them and the response was, "Wow. You have twenty-four of those?" The shops have gotten a little better about all that now. I think there were just so many years when they never had to buy anything. They were still using those

---

6. In order to have computerized control at the front end, the back end—the dimmers—also needed to be electronic.
7. A 6 X 16 Ellipsoidal Reflector Spotlight (ERS) is designed for medium to long throws upwards of 40 to 50 feet. A 6 X 22 is designed for even longer throw distances.

[same] piano boards that they were using in 1932. All of a sudden, they had to make these huge forays into the bank to buy new equipment.

Abe Feder, when he designed *My Fair Lady*, used autotransformer piano boards as opposed to resistance dimmers. There were 3K plates and 6K plates, but they were autotransformers. *My Fair Lady* was such an enormous hit, in the scope of what we would think of *Phantom of the Opera* now, that if a theatre wanted *My Fair Lady*, they had to convert to alternating current. Even when *My Fair Lady* was most popular, it never played more than two weeks in a town—it would come back many times and it traveled by rail, so all the road houses in America converted to AC. Whereas the Mark Hellinger Theatre in New York was the only one that ever converted to AC because it was where *My Fair Lady* was playing. As time moved on, if a production wanted alternating current, they probably had to pay for it.

Alternating current was also available at the Uris Theatre when Jane Reisman designed there in 1974. In this instance, as she explained, the control system was a ten-scene preset board, rather than the otherwise ubiquitous road boards found elsewhere on Broadway.

REISMAN: I did do a show on Broadway that had a ten-scene preset board. But it was the first issue. The reason we were able to do it was that it wasn't just one show—it was a season for the Nederlander Company at the Uris Theatre, now the Gershwin Theatre, where they brought in a concert performance either every week or every two weeks. Most of them ran for two weeks. There were about ten different performances over the year—it was about six months or seven months. Every two weeks there was a changeover. There were usually two different groups that came into the theatre in the usual concert tour way, where they might show up at noon or they might show up at 6:00. Maybe they would show up at 7:30 at night on Tuesday, and then run for two weeks. Sometimes it was an advance man who would come and know what they needed, or what they wanted. Sometimes I would have a program of what numbers came where on a play list, but quite often I didn't even have that. But they would freeze the show by 7:00 before opening. Our solution for it was really to have some kind of looks programmed, or there was no way we were going to be able to make this happen. This was in the days before rock-and-roll boards, and all that stuff we have now. We did this in fall 1974. I think it was the last week in September. There was a problem though, because there had never been any non-piano board on Broadway at that time, and therefore the shops didn't own any. So we had to find a board with a bug[8] on it. The only board we could find, after a lot of research, was in Imero Fiorentino's studio . . . his company that did TV projects and a lot of event lighting had some boards that they had either had manufactured for them or put together themselves, and they were bug boards. So we were able to rent a ten-scene preset board for the season from them. At that time I believe that was the only IA bug board in the Broadway area. That show went in in late September or October 1974. And I believe Tharon Musser got *A Chorus Line*'s computer a year later.

LE: A Chorus Line *opened in fall 1975.*

REISMAN: So as far as we know, mine was the first preset board on Broadway. And at that time, there really wasn't a choice of computer board. Also, financially, this was the way to do it . . . we were able to have one operator . . .

MITCH DANA: We were using a five-scene preset at BAM [Brooklyn Academy of Music] when we did *Joseph and the Amazing Technicolor Dreamcoat,* and I think that was seventy-two channels wide, and then we had an auxiliary twenty-four-pack that was a two-scene. It was lots of fun. Shirley Pendergast and I taped the show, and we then played the show back with the stage manager's calls for the operator, because the operator couldn't figure out how to do the presets and so on. So we ran the show three times by playing it on tape and standing there and say-ing, "Whoops, that's wrong, stop." And then I had to have Shirley go over and say, "No, here's where you set this and here's where you do that," and the one operator's hands literally had to be located for virtu-ally everything. It was very frustrating.

REISMAN: When I was teaching at Emerson there was still the old, little

---

8. The "bug" referred to here is the stamp of the International Alliance of Theatrical Stage Employees (IATSE), the stage hands' union.

preset board up in there, the little six-thing board in the student theatre. They're still around. I just saw one in a theatre the other day. It was a Century thing, what was it called? I can't remember the name. That little tiny portable preset board was in lots of places. But certainly the Broadway thing was the last thing that happened, not where it started.

But at that same time we [Reisman and husband Neil Peter Jampolis] had been using somewhat computerized boards—nothing like what we use today—in opera houses all over the country . . . Tulsa Opera, which was in a new opera house in Tulsa that opened in '74 or '73. We had an early Kliegl computer board—Memo-Q or Q-File. But it was an interesting problem house because it was the first house we ever worked in that was dimmer-per-circuit, but there was no soft patching.[9] It actually got to be very funny, because I worked for the opera there over many, many years. If you were working with a director you hadn't worked with before, he must have thought you were nuts when you asked for channel 256 and channel 370, and it went up to channel 700, through the opera house. There was no soft patching and so the only way you could cope was to write cues and file cues in the back that lumped all your systems together. . . . There was no way to do groups or anything like that, so we used to write cues like all the blue cyc top and bottom and all the blue sidelights, like today we might do with groups. Then you just call for that cue to pile on. We had an extraordinary electrician working there in that house, which made working there just a joy. His name was Joe Jack and he was a legend there; unfortunately he's not alive any more. He was in a drowning accident . . .

Cincinnati Playhouse had a board on tape, I think it was also Kliegl. It was like a tape player. Once it failed you had to check all this cassette-type tape. And that was in '73, '72. But by the time *A Chorus Line* happened on Broadway, we had all been using computers.

DANA: I remember working at ACT on a four-scene preset Edkatron board. We all played that game. I think the first time I really used a computer was somewhere in Los Angeles or San Francisco, but I remember one particular time, which was Seattle. It was based on the old Sweet 16.

---

9. "Soft patching" is the process whereby dimmers are assigned to channels of control to be "memorized" by the computer control console.

I can't remember who made that.[10] It'll come to me after a while. It was a man who made computers and boards in Los Angeles and was one of those kind of crazy genius types. Anyway, I was designing *History of the American Film*; in fact I did another show up there, too. But it had a lot of effects, and those were the days when the memory lines were identified with a number. This board had 256 [cue] memories. And they were numbered 1 through 256. You couldn't insert cues, you couldn't do anything, so if you wanted to insert a cue and if you had numbered consecutively, you had to go from 1 to, say 201, and link them, and then link 201 back to 2. And if you made a change in 1 or 201 or 2, then you lost all the links. So you had to go back and relink everything. Very confusing. And with a special-effects show, where you wanted to run a whole bunch of cues in a line, with follows, it became very confusing and difficult to figure out where things were going to be.

■

Although clearly not the first computer control console, the computer that made its way to Broadway on *A Chorus Line* was historically significant. Its very existence proved to producers and rental houses that the capital investment necessary to change over to electronic dimming and control was financially viable. Furthermore, the extremely successful application of the console to the lighting design showcased the aesthetic possibilities of computerized control.

OSTERMANN: One reason I think that Tharon Musser got *A Chorus Line* on a computer was that there were so many cues in the show that were snap cues—they were all bumps. I would say 80 percent of the cues, maybe even 90 percent of those light cues, were bumps. But anybody seeing that show almost didn't notice the lighting because the cues happened so perfectly with the music and with the script that they were unnoticeable, just like a great edit is in a movie. I knew that show really well, and those bump cues are what made the lighting work. That's why we needed computers. There is no way that those cues could have been run on manual road boards. The hearsay is that Tharon actually

---

10. The Sweet 16 was another Van Buren–designed product.

tried to do some cues on a road board to show the stagehands' union (the IA) that it was going to be impossible.

RICHARD WINKLER: The reason that Gordon Pearlman's organization was chosen—and there was another organization, and I believe it was Kliegl but I'm not sure—was that Gordon guaranteed it. And the other organization, the other business could not. So, that's why Tharon went with Gordon.

LE: *And he was with EDI [Electronics Diversified, Inc.] at the time?*

WINKLER: Yes, that's right. And it was a fascinating process.

GORDON PEARLMAN: This console was not developed for EDI originally. I was teaching at the University of North Carolina in Chapel Hill and developed the console on a grant at the University. Subsequently, I went to work for EDI and took the console design along with me. In those days software belonged to the author, not the university. . . . Those days have changed.

The console was designed on a PDP-8 Digital Equipment Company computer. It was completely designed and working at the University of North Carolina before it ever went to EDI. The problem was that at Chapel Hill they didn't have electronic dimmers. This was the days of autotransformers as the primary source of dimming. We had one six-pack of dimmers and we played with it on that for six or eight months before I went to EDI. Some of the electronics were redesigned at EDI, but that's about all.

LE: *At Chapel Hill, you were on the faculty in the theatre department?*

PEARLMAN: Yes, I was an assistant professor, the lighting designer, and technical director.

LE: *Was the LS-8 the first console that you developed, or had you been working on others before that?*

PEARLMAN: No, this was the first console I developed.

LE: *And did you have computer training?*

PEARLMAN: No.

LE: *You just dove in?*

PEARLMAN: No. The joke was that you got two things for free at UNC when you were on the faculty: You either got the gym or the computer center.

LE: *And you took the computer center?*

PEARLMAN: How I got into that was that one of the graduate students was doing a production where he had 35-millimeter slide projectors and was controlling them with a paper tape reader, which we picked up surplus at the state surplus store. We quickly discovered that if we wanted to make a change in the order of the show, we had to repunch the entire tape. In those days it was a Teletype that was then connected to the computer center. I went out and taught myself enough BASIC programming to be able to write the cues in this BASIC program and then have it repunch the paper tape in the Teletype. It took an hour to an hour and a half to repunch the tape, but at least every time you wanted to make a change you didn't have to go and manually repunch the whole thing. You could edit changes into the middle, and then get the Teletype to repunch a paper tape for you.

LE: *I've been trying to find specifications for the LS-8, or some written information on what kind of features it had, and I haven't found anything.*

PEARLMAN: I don't know if I have it written any more. I could certainly tell you most everything. It was 125 control channels. There was no [soft] patching in those days so it had 125 dimmers as well; it had an A-B cross-fader pair and a C-D cross-fader pair that could be manual or be timed. Basically, they were always used in the time mode, although *A Chorus Line* ran it, as I remember, on the manual cross-fader pair, where they actually pushed those handles back and forth. There was a tremendous amount of reticence about letting the computer take over too much of the show. They felt that the operator had to be in control, and I think that most of it was in fact run on the manual cross-fader pair. . . . It didn't have much else, to tell you the truth.

LE: *I spoke at length with Mitch Dana, who told me he had the second LS-8 at ACT in San Francisco, and he said he used it as a database manager for his paperwork.*

PEARLMAN: Well, it was a PDP-8 so it was the equivalent of today's PC.

Mitch Dana explained how he maximized the capabilities of this early control console.

DANA: Dirk Epperson, my assistant, and I sat down to try and figure out what we would want as a computer board if we had one, and we put out the parameters for what we wanted. Then Dirk saw the EDI board at a conference and thought that would do exactly what it was that was required. Tharon Musser used that board on *A Chorus Line*. That was board number 1, and we had serial number 2. The reason we got number 2 was that she went into production two weeks before we did. Dirk had written his thesis when he was at Yale on using triac dimmers—on putting the dimmers on the pipe . . . like our "intelligent dimming" today.[11]

We used that LS-8 for database management; we did everything on that LS-8. That was the best of them all, and it was the culmination of where we had been at that stage of the game. There was a whole series of things we loved. First of all, you could insert point cues, so inserting cues was easy. You didn't have to write cues as 1, 5, 10, 15, leaving room for inserts and then do strange links when you ran out of cue numbers. That was quite a wonderful kind of thing to have. But what we really loved about it was that for the first time, we could compensate for a filament. If you had the bare light bulb on stage and you were bumping because somebody turned the light switch on, and you wanted the bare light bulb to be at 50 percent and then all other lights were also going to be at 50 percent, you got a double bump. The filament of the light bulb arrived before the light from all the stage lights, and we found ourselves very quickly writing point cues, where in a 0 count the filament of the light bulb went to 20 percent or 30 percent. Then, along with all of the lights that were supposedly boosting it, the cue had an automatic follow in two-tenths of a second to take it to the level you wanted; that way everything arrived at the same time. That was really a wonderful, wonderful thing—instead of having that double bump look. The

11. Coincidentally, the "Intelligent Power System" line of dimmers was developed by Gordon Pearlman for his company, Rosco/Entertainment Technology.

other thing we liked was being able to do reverse cross-fades. In the early computer boards you could do a cross-fade, and you could do a pile-on, but you couldn't really do one where the up time was slower than the down time.

We really liked that LS-8. I really thought that was a wonderful board because Dirk Epperson knew enough to program it properly. He set up the database off of it. At ACT we put in our inventory. We put in my light plot from the beginning. We hung circuits every place, and instead of using unit numbers we used position numbers on pipes, because with up to eight shows being in the rep at any one time, if you used a unit number it was going to change the next time you put something in, so we used the position number and hung units on position numbers. Essentially you had a large empty instrument schedule, and you hung stuff in it. After a while I would take the instrument schedule and I'd be in Chicago someplace, and I'd do the light plot for the next show based on the instrument schedule, because I knew where there were openings. There's an opening left of center, there's an opening right of center, and so on. Then I would just send in the list, and everybody would hang it and hook it up, and it was very simple. But once you hung a unit there, if Dirk then entered it into the database, it then subtracted instruments from the instrument inventory, doing that kind of database management. It would automatically compare stuff, so that when we put in show five, we could then print new paperwork for one through four, and it would give us all the changes.

LE: *I didn't realize that it had that capability.*

DANA: It was a full computer. It was an LS-8 instead of an electronic computer-like system that was dedicated to lighting, which is what everything else had been. The comparison would be to a 486 computer, so you could do things with it. It wasn't dedicated to one item. It wasn't used that way by many people, because most people weren't good enough at programming to actually get in and do that. But Dirk was, and as a result he made our life at ACT so easy. I can't give him enough credit. The man's a good designer and he really knows his computer stuff, and he's a good friend. And he's just . . . one of the best assistants I've ever had in my entire lifetime, as well as a true colleague.

It is interesting to note that Gordon Pearlman's more recently designed control system, Horizon, operates on a similar principle by using his specialized software on a Windows-based PC with an additional hardware device to send out the appropriate control signal to the dimmers.

PEARLMAN: [The LS-8] had 16K—not meg—16K of core memory. And that included all the keystroke storage and all of the program storage. This was 16K of 12-bit words. And it was core memory. By today's standards, that's nothing—your desktop calculator probably has a hundred times that in it.

LE: *Was there something that preceded the LS-8? Was there an LS-7 or an LS-6?*

PEARLMAN: Well, no. When I went to EDI they had come out with a 16K board—we had an 8K board—so we were able to put more memory in it. Originally the only way to load the program was off of the paper tape, which took forty-five minutes. First you had to toggle in the first sixteen instructions by hand. That gave it enough smarts to read a little bit of paper tape, which then told the machine how to read the whole program, which it would then do. The miracle of all times is that the original machine ran continuously. We installed the machine in July of '75, and the first four months it ran without ever having to reload the program, because there really was no way to reload the program . . . besides having to call Steve Terry up at home and having him run over to reload it, because he wasn't working on the show at that time. From there we went to a machine that had a disk drive on it.

LE: *I read in an old* Theatre Crafts *article that Tharon Musser had wanted to use one of the earlier EDI consoles. I'm wondering what you had to do to try to convince her to try this one.*

PEARLMAN: Well . . . that's a fun story, too. I had just moved to Portland with my family from Chapel Hill with two little tiny kids and was supposed to work on July the 15th, if I remember the date correctly, and somewhere around July 8th or 9th somebody was knocking at the front door—we didn't have a telephone yet. It was Paul Bennett, the president of EDI at that time (and still is), telling me that they had sold a console to a Broadway show—he didn't know the name of the Broadway show—and they couldn't build it. They promised it and promised it and were working on the design, but they couldn't get it to work, so they were going to have to deliver one of my consoles. Now understand, EDI had never built one of my consoles. I had built the one in Chapel Hill, but they had never built one. We built one for a trade show, but it didn't actually drive dimmers. So, working night and day, literally, for forty-eight straight hours, Steve Carlson, who works with us here at Rosco/ET, and I built a console, put it on an airplane, and flew it to New York forty-eight hours later. . . . By that time I knew it was *A Chorus Line*, I knew exactly what we were talking about. *Chorus Line* had already been a big hit down at the Public and was moving uptown, and everybody was talking about it. So that's how the LS-8 ended up on *Chorus Line*. It was not Tharon's choice, per se. She had been convinced that EDI was going to build her what was basically a manual console that could remember; it wasn't going to be CRT-based or any of those things that the LS-8 turned out to be. That's how it got there, and it was a kind of a miracle that it ever got built at all. And the big miracle was that it ran for four months without trouble, and then we replaced it with a console that had printed circuit boards in it and things like that . . .

To continue the story—I flew to New York with the console with the assumption that I would spend a day or two there and install it, and then I would come home. Well, Tharon wouldn't let me leave. So I spent two weeks in New York, basically just watching rehearsals, sitting beside Tharon. It was fascinating. I was a young lighting designer at University of North Carolina, and I thought this was wonderful. My wife was not exactly overjoyed with small children in a strange town where she knew absolutely no one, where we'd lived for about two days before I left. I had pulled a bathroom out before I left and was starting to do some technical director-type stuff in it, putting in new appliances and things, so she was not overjoyed. And I kept saying to Tharon over and over again, "Tharon, I have got to go." And I had dinner with Tharon and Gary Shevett[12] every evening, saying, "Tharon, I have got to go home.

---

12. Shevett was the production electrician.

My wife is just crazy back there." And she's saying, "No, no, you can't go until the show opens." So Tharon said, "OK, we'll fly your wife out for opening night." Remember, I was a $10,000-a-year college professor before I went to work for EDI. Actually, it was Gary Shevett, the master electrician's, idea. And they did it. She did come out for opening night and it was great fun. We all went to Sardi's afterwards with Tharon and it was wonderful fun. The sidelight to the story is they never did pay me back for my wife's coming to New York. Every time I'd see Frank DeVerna[13] for years after that—we were still doing business together—I reminded him that he still owes me the $300 airfare [laughter].

LE: _Once it was up and running on Broadway, did you get feedback from Tharon, or from Richard Winkler, or . . ._

PEARLMAN: There wasn't anybody to say "wouldn't it be nice if it did this, wouldn't it be nice if it did that," because nobody had any concept of what you could or couldn't do with one of these things. They had come from a ten-scene preset at the Public, and a ten-scene preset was magic to them. . . . I mean, across the street people were running piano boards on _Grease._ They had thirty dimmers and they thought that was a lot, so it wasn't just that it was the first computer.

WINKLER: I remember being on the headset at one point and Gordon said, "Well, what should we call this function?" And I said, "Gee, Gordon, I don't know, what does this function do?" And he explained it to me, and I named it. And we did that a few more times.

LE: _And what was that function?_

WINKLER: It was something called "Load." There were load numbers and memory numbers on the original computer, which were not the same. I actually have the original track sheet to prove it. And the most interesting thing is, when I look back at those original track sheets, they were not set up the way the screen was set up.

LE: _Who knew to do that at the time?_

---

13. Then owner and president of Four Star Stage Lighting, the lighting equipment supplier.

WINKLER: Exactly. We were the first people to use a memory board on the street. And . . . we were just all finding our way with it.

LE: *When the show moved uptown, were there changes made to the design because there was more flexibility?*

WINKLER: Yes. Specifically what I can recall is that the "thought lights," [soliloquy specials] were on A-B switches downtown, and they were individual uptown.[14]

LE: *That made it easier?*

WINKLER: Yes, I can remember that very specifically.

LE: *That theatre was still using A-B switches in 1986 when I was assisting Arden Fingerhut in there. Did the cuing change with the change in control system?*

WINKLER: The cuing was exactly the same uptown as it was downtown.

LE: *Was there a noticeable difference in execution, or was that a transparent change as well?*

WINKLER: We had two really good operators downtown, on the preset board. A guy by the name of Julie . . . whose last name I can no longer remember.

LE: *Julie retired a few years ago.*

WINKLER: And a woman by the name of Sara Schrager who now does other stuff, primarily architectural lighting. They were great. Everything was always there.

The most interesting story, or one of the most interesting stories about *A Chorus Line* and the memory board, is the story of the afternoon when someone, who shall remain nameless, put 210 volts through the system. This was after we were uptown on Broadway. It fried everything. I remember getting a phone call—it was ten days or so after we had opened on Broadway—we had had a cleanup call in the afternoon

---

14. When a dimmer is split into A-B "sides," only one of the two lights in the dimmer can be on at a time.

for a Saturday matinee. Or, we were uptown for some other specific reason. It was about 6:00 in the evening. Tharon and I had each gone home (we lived around the corner from each other at that time). I was on the phone with my best friend, and the call was interrupted by the operator, and it was Tharon saying that the board had crashed. I still had all the paperwork in my briefcase, since I had just walked in the door. She said, "The board is crashed, get uptown as fast as you can. I'll meet you there." So I hopped into a cab and got uptown. The memory part of the board was gone.

That evening we did the show on the preset board backup . . . and in the booth at the Shubert Theatre were Jeff Hamlin [the stage manager], myself, Tharon, Marilyn Rennagel, Dermot Lynch [house electrician], and Gary Shevett. (That was not in order of importance.) Tharon and I shared the cuing bible. . . . She asked me to suggest to her what cues should be cut and what cues should not be cut, so that I was talking to her and to Jeff at the same time. And she was feeding the dimmer numbers—all of a sudden they weren't channel numbers any more, they were dimmer numbers—to Gary, Dermot, and Marilyn, and they were moving the preset sliders up and down. Jeff and I were talking to each other, and I said, "All right, we don't need this cue, we don't need that cue." I just kept handing Tharon pieces of cue sheets for the ones we were going to do. This was an evening that Tharon and I shared together in tandem and in absolute terror. I remember getting to the cue that was the "Paul's monologue" cue, which was nothing but a single follow spot at full. Tharon and I just melted onto the floor together, because of the stress and the pressure. . . . It was truly a moment, it was truly a moment—those hours, during the show, those two hours and ten minutes or two hours and seven minutes, were the most terrifying thing that I have ever experienced in the theatre. Because here we had this big hit show with a packed house and we didn't have the control that we had always had. And it was sick, and it was terrifying. . . . No one, as I recall, in the union [IATSE] knew how to solve this problem and fix it quickly, because everything was so new. The guys just didn't know how to solve these problems instantly, and so that's when Steve Terry, who was not in the union at the time, was called in. And Steve Terry fixed the board.

TERRY: It actually goes kind of like this: I had been working for the Dance Theatre of Harlem for five and a half years on tour in the U.S. and Europe. Gary Fails and I were on the tour together. (Gary Fails is the president of City Theatrical now, famous for things like Source 4 accessories.) When Dance Theatre of Harlem had been doing New York seasons, I met a Local 1 electrician who worked on the show named Gary Shevett. Gary was the production electrician on *A Chorus Line*. One day I went up to visit him, thinking, "Well, maybe I'd like to get involved in working on Broadway." I remember walking into that theatre where they had just put the first computer on. It was just after the show had opened, and I happened to be at the theatre, and the thing had blown up.

WINKLER: There were half a dozen of us, or eight of us involved in this crisis. It was truly a moment in theatre history. I am very honored that I was there and I was very lucky that I was there. . . . We got through the show on Saturday night. At that point in time we were not playing Sunday matinees, and Monday morning—I'm sure we all went out and got blasted Saturday—Monday morning at 9 o'clock, Steve was in the theatre. Steve was in the theatre Monday morning. And I don't remember if we got it fixed for Monday night, or not until Tuesday night. That I do not recall. But I do remember going into the theatre on Monday.

TERRY: They were frantically looking around for someone who had a vacuum-powered solder sucker and had the knowledge to suck out forty dead ICs. The original LS-8 was designed at the University of North Carolina by Gordon Pearlman. He would probably be the first one to admit, and I would certainly back it up, that it was the most marginal design you've ever seen in your life, from a hardware point of view. He used a Digital Equipment PDP-8A computer, but it had a lot of other PC boards hung on it. These were all the latest technology: large-scale analog multiplexers, but if you just looked sideways at them, they blew up. So this thing had been blown up. They called me in because I happened to be there and because I was a kind of New York source for this type of electronics stuff. So, I spent a few days helping them fix it. Then I got a job as a substitute electrician on the show, and I took over the responsibility for the maintenance of that LS-8. The first one that was there was actually the prototype, and it was later replaced by a production model. Then I went on to be the soundman for the show, working for Otts Munderloh, and that was a long stint, ending in about 1982 or so.

The LS-8 was . . . well, we thought it was the most marvelous product around. And it was, for its day, compared to the other stuff that had been out there: the Memo-Q or Sweet 16, or any of that stuff coming out of the George Van Buren–Strand camp, such as System 128.

LE: *What was the Van Buren–Strand connection at that time?*

TERRY: The stuff coming out of Strand in England was this big MMS drum memory system. Martin Moore was the chief engineer at Strand during the period that they did "Light Board" for Richard Pilbrow, and he was at Strand for a long period before that. Sweet 16, System 128, and Compuset 2000 were the boards that they had done with Van Buren. There was a big panic on *Chorus Line* because Steve Skirpan, inventor of Autocue, had sued EDI and gotten an injunction against people using the LS-8. It was based on a patent for a memory lighting control with a video display. It was a very weak patent, but meanwhile everybody was really scared. Tours were going out. The international and the national companies were getting ready to go out on tour, so something had to be done. So Tharon basically called her friend Chuck Levy at Strand and said, "Chuck, what are we going to do here?" And I think then they reeled in Dave Cunningham and that whole crowd. And I'm not really clear here what or how the jump was made from Van Buren. I think Dave Cunningham had worked at Van Buren but now was with Strand. So they produced Multi-Q, and Multi-Q was the console that then went out on tour with all the *Chorus Line* companies. It was halfway between a Kliegl Performance and an LS-8.

LE: *Did your involvement with Production Arts begin at around the same time?*

TERRY: In April of 1976 I got fed up with touring with Dance Theatre of Harlem. I had actually designed and built a lot of touring equipment for them while I was there. My friends John McGraw and Peter Forward had this little company called Production Arts Lighting around the corner on East Tenth Street. Peter Forward had been a professor of mine in my six-month span of going to college. Actually, I left college six months after I went in to go on tour with Dance Theatre of Harlem. Peter was teaching a stagecraft course and I said to myself, "I can pick up three credits here." Through a long series of events, I ended up taking a pay cut from Dance Theatre of Harlem to go work for Production Arts Lighting, then in something like 3,000 square feet down on East Tenth Street.

LE: *How far we've come in twenty years. It's really pretty amazing.*

TERRY: Gordon and Steve actually left EDI and went to work for Kliegl, so the LS-8 became a real orphan until they removed it. When they removed it, I actually saved it, stuck it in the basement of Production Arts in New York. And then Gordon called me and said, "You know, we'd kind of like to have that in our conference room. Ship it out here, will you?" And so I did, after a couple years.

LE: *Where is that original console now?*

PEARLMAN: The console was in the Computer Museum in Boston. They called me and asked me if they could have it (I had it at the time). And I told them that it worked. They said, "Oh, no, no, we don't want to hear that. Please, do not send it to us in working condition. We would just feel obligated to keep it working." So basically sitting under the console is a Great American Access, which is also a console which we built, actually running the lights.

TERRY: The Computer Museum in Boston is now closed. The unit is in the collection of the new Computer Museum History Center at Moffatt Field, California. It's just a very clever little exhibit, which we donated a bunch of lights for. It's a set of a backstage area with the board operator sitting at the board operating the show.

LE TO MITCH DANA: *Did you have any problems with the LS-8 console you used at ACT?*

DANA: No. We didn't really have any problems. . . . Well . . . we had our problems. I remember one cue setting session, I think it was *Othello*, and it was the first or second show that we had used that console on. It was late at night and I called back to my board operator Rich Moustie, and I said, "OK, let's get out, let's close it up." I heard this godawful . . . noise come from the room. And then he went, "Oh, shit." I said, "All right, so what happened?" He had taken the disk out, in order to make sure that he didn't overwrite it and cause problems when he was running for safety, and so he had now dumped the board, and all the information was now gone from the board. We had been in one of those sessions where you're lighting on the fly, and good things were happening, but it was thirty-five minutes to an hour's worth of concentrated, really solid work with no breaks, where they were just running it on stage and we were working as fast as we could. It looked gorgeous—oh, God, it looked good—but we hadn't saved anything for thirty-five minutes, and all of it just went away. So Rich called me on headset. He said, "Well, I think I screwed that up . . . could you stay late tonight?" I said, "Yeah?" He said, "Well, we just lost all this information, would you remember it if you stayed?" I said, "I don't know if I can remember it, but I can come close if we keep it fresh." He said "OK," and we sent everybody home, and he and I sat down and reprogrammed the show that night, till 3:00 in the morning. He was an IA man but he did not ask for pay for that night.

LE: *What happened to Dirk Epperson, your assistant and programmer?*

DANA: He formed a company that does box office systems.[15] The next thing that ended up happening with that LS-8 that we had was that it started running our box office at ACT. The only problem was that the box office couldn't run while we were running a rehearsal.

TERRY: Subsequently, Gordon Pearlman and Steve Carlson went off to develop the Performance for Kliegl, and then the Performer for Kliegl.

OSTERMANN: The great thing about Tharon Musser was that even though she got the computers on Broadway in 1975 with *Chorus Line*, we did, I would say, ten box set shows after that, on Broadway, where she still used resistance boards. She did not need a computer to do them. She was very efficient; she only used computer control when it was necessary. She tried out all the different computers. I remember we worked with Multi-Q's; we worked with Light Palette. I think Tharon was involved with the design of the Light Palette at the beginning in that she

---

15. Epperson went on to found "ObjectSwitch," a company affiliated with Sybase, a computing resources firm.

said, "When you bring a handle up on a resistance board, it stays there until you tell the electricians to bring it down." That was the whole point of tracking consoles. We did *1940s Radio Hour* on a brand new Light Palette in 1979. We had 104 4K dimmers on that, controlled by a Light Palette. Just previously, I had assisted John Gleason on [the revival of] *My Fair Lady* in 1976 with six resistance boards. In those three years, that was a big progression. Multi-Q, Micro-Q, Kliegl Performers, Kliegl Performer II's, we went through all those kinds of boards. . . . I don't remember the Q-File. That was a big board in Las Vegas at the time. We didn't have that many in New York. It used to be it was whatever Four Star owned in stock.

■

LE TO KEN BILLINGTON: *What was your first Broadway show on which you used a computer?*

BILLINGTON: As you know, the first show on Broadway that used a computer was *A Chorus Line*; the second computer used on Broadway was me. It's sort of an interesting story here. I was being a successful designer. The only computer was sitting at, of course, *A Chorus Line*. They had their share of problems with it, for whatever reasons—static electricity or whatever it was, and there was no backup or any of that. And I was doing a lot of road companies at the time and I had gotten Production Arts to develop a five-scene preset touring production console which I was using on road companies of *My Fair Lady* and some other shows, and then Hal Prince called and asked me to design a show called *Side by Side by Sondheim*. It was a musical review and I had seen it in London, actually, just because I had been there and seen it, not because I knew I was going to light it in New York. It's a show that needed a lot of cues. It could clearly be done on piano boards but it would have taken, with the cyc lighting and all, probably five boards—which would have meant three operators—and the general manager was not about to pay for that. He only wanted to pay for one operator. I probably could have gotten him to two, but he didn't want to do that. So then I started thinking, "Hmm, what could I do? Let me start looking around for preset boards." So I started looking at preset consoles. Now this is 1977, or maybe '76. I'm looking around and preset boards exist but they're bulky, and so I thought, "What about memory consoles?" There were really only like two manufacturers of them around—Kliegl and Century Strand. I called Kliegl and they were very nice to me and said, "Oh, we'll send you a brochure." This was when the Performer I was coming around, but it wasn't really finished yet. And I thought, "Well, that sort of blew that." And then I called Century Lighting—I'm thinking they were Century Strand in those days. I got Wally [Russell] on the phone and Wally said, "Oh, sure. We got a board here for you." And I said, "Oh, great." And instead of saying they would send me a catalog, they said, "What time do you want a car to pick you up? We'll show it to you." So I said I could get myself there and so they said, "When?" And I said, "Tomorrow," and they said, "What time?" and I said, "10:00" and they said, "Absolutely— you can stay here as long as you want."

So I got in a car and I went out to New Jersey, wherever Century was at the time, and there was Wally and all the executives from Century Lighting with the Multi-Q, which hadn't really been used anyplace yet. They had the demo there. They brought Marcia Madeira in to demonstrate the board to me. She was working for them at the time. This was rudimentary memory lighting with no video monitors. You had to push pots up to get the level. This was the board they were using on the road companies of *Chorus Line,* but it had not made it any further than the road companies of *Chorus Line,* and *Chorus Line* was thought of as a special animal so it wasn't automatic that if *Chorus Line* has it, everybody can have it. Lighting hadn't made it to that level in those days. But it was proven and it was working out on the road with *Chorus Line.* So they showed it to me and I wanted it for a Broadway show but, of course, I needed to buy dimmers, too. Nobody had electronic dimmers for the Broadway rental market. So to take the console meant having to buy dimmers, too. I figured I needed forty-two dimmers. I figured this out— they were all 4K dimmers and I said to them, after about three hours and thinking this was great, I said, "I want to use this, so I better get some numbers from you for the console and forty-two dimmers." And they came back and said, "Oh, thirteen." I'm making this number up, but it was in the neighborhood of $13,000. Clearly numbers that were so far off of what the reality was—the console at the time was selling for around $27,000. I called the general manager because Four Star would not buy the console or the dimmers. So I called Hal Prince, who was producing the show, and I said, "I want to do this." And he said, "How much does it cost?" and I said, "$13,000," and he said, "OK. Is this a good console?" And I said, "This is the best in the world." And they purchased it. The producer purchased the console and we brought it into the Music Box Theatre. Marcia Madeira came along to teach Jimmy Maloney, the head electrician, how to operate it. We sat out front and I lit the entire production of *Side by Side by Sondheim* in about six hours. The general manager later said to me, "You know, that thing paid for itself in crew time." Those were the sorts of shows where you would have to do three days of run-throughs just so they could routine the boards.

The console worked, and in that timeframe, I think every stagehand and every general manager in New York City walked backstage and stood next to this guy and watched him push his lever back and forth . . . and that was the beginning. After that, within one year, I would say 60 percent of the shows were on memory control. And within two years, everything except something that was really old—like *Grease*—was all on memory control. They were all on the same console. And that was interesting in that Strand did a very smart marketing thing. They made this console available almost for free for the Broadway theatre. I always wondered if Kliegl had sent a car to me to go out and look at that board first, would the Kliegl Performer have won the Broadway race? Of course, ultimately the Strand console became the legitimate theatre's console of choice, not the Kliegl consoles. So that's a little bit of history there.[16]

I do remember doing a musical on Broadway in the late '70s called *But Never Jam Today*—it was a black version of *Alice in Wonderland*—and we were in the Longacre Theatre, and the Longacre Theatre was still a DC [direct current] theatre. It had some alternating current but not enough to run an entire musical. So I had all my front area lights on resistance dimmers—piano boards—and next to this board I had a Q-Level or some Strand console that ran all the overheads and side lights, so the man would hit the button on the board and then push the dimmers up.

DENNIS PARICHY: The first show I was tempted to use a memory board on was *The Water Engine*, if I remember correctly. We moved it from

---

16. Kliegl filed for bankruptcy in the early 1990s and eventually shut down operations.

downtown, at the Public Theatre, up to the Plymouth. It had been forty-eight dimmers and needed to be ninety-six or something of that sort. It was right about then that all that stuff was beginning to appear, and I hadn't used any of those boards previously. We went through a whole hassle of, "How are we going to do this one? Can I get . . . ?" I don't even remember what board we were attempting to get. We had one of those situations in which we went back and forth and said, "What has the shop got? What can we get? How can we do this?" And what we ended up with was a really peculiar thing, where about half the show was on a memory board and the other half of the show was being run on a preset board. It was very complicated and just a crazy situation, because we didn't know what was going to be available until the very last moment. I don't really remember much about that except that it was just messy getting the whole show in, and I guess I really wasn't sure just how the hell those boards worked or anything at that point. Just prior to that I had done *Best Little Whorehouse* which ended up, several years later, being one of the last two shows on resistance boards running on Broadway. It played downtown for a while and then went away and on tour and came back and was still on resistance boards. And there was a point at which we were sort of debating would my show or another show, which one of us would be first to close; which would be the last show with those old boards.

DANA: In the early boards, one of the major problems we all had was: what if you're doing a Vegas-style show, and it's the last minute and you need to put the show in but you haven't got time to sit down and punch all these numbers in and go to each of the looks? So early on Kliegl had the market there, because they manufactured boards with sub-boards, essentially with a pot for each dimmer. You could have a board with seventy-two pots on it, but once you set the pots, you could then record the setup by just saying "record cue 23." Then you could reach your hand out, change the pot, go on to the next thing; much like we do with a Producer board or any of those now. The result was that you could work on the fly, but if you came across a look you really liked, you could record it as a cue and then fill in the programming in between. If you were very last minute, you could do what roadies in rock and roll do a lot, which is you could play it live. You can't do that with an Obsession or Light Palette; it's almost impossible. And so Kliegl had the run on that kind of thing for quite a while. But of course, because the board was not a last-action board,[17] it was recording everything at every time, so you knew exactly how many cues you could have. If there were 250 cues and 125 channels on your board, then you could do 125 channels times 250 cues, or whatever, and that was the total amount of information that you could get. Naturally, with a last-action board, you can't tell that, because you may only be using one channel in one cue, and you have 250 other information spaces available that can be thrown anywhere. So you really can't tell what the upper limit of an Obsession is, because it depends on how the board is being used. If you haven't got multiple parts, if you haven't got multiple groups, if you haven't got lots of sub-masters and effects and so on, that board's range is extended almost infinitum. So at the time, Kliegl had the run on all of that live performance type stuff, and Strand was getting the lead on all of the more theatrical things, more planned operations.

WEISS: For industrial shows the Q-Level was great because you could number the presets so that you could make it up as you went along if you had to, with all of the torm lights in the right-hand buttons one through nine, and then the left-hand buttons represented in-1 left, in-2 left, and so on. So you punch the right two buttons and get the red torms in-2. The Kliegl Performer was the first straight play/preset-style memory board I used. Playback was more consistent than ever before, but the tape backup failed frequently.

JAMPOLIS: Around 1976 I began working in Ottawa at the National Arts Centre, lighting operas, and they had . . . what would it have been called? Maybe a Memo-Q, or Q-Level . . . that was the first time I got to do big productions with a memory board.

LE: *You mentioned earlier that you didn't care for the preset board way of thinking, but that first memory system you used in Ottawa, the Q-Level, was like a preset board, if I remember correctly.*

JAMPOLIS: It was. So I would always copy the cue over into the next cue

---

17. "Last action" means a tracking-style console such as the Strand Light Palette or ETC Obsession.

and keep going, and then go back and prewarm . . . I would do all the things I could to make the thing move.

I remember perhaps the first show I did on one of those boards—it was the opera *A Midsummer Night's Dream*. And there is a line in *Midsummer Night's Dream,* "The seasons alter." I guess it's Oberon or Titania singing . . . chiding, with the spring, the summer . . . and the director wanted some indication of this because it was magic and they were waving wands around, and he wanted the stage to be summer, winter, spring, whatever. He had never worked with a designer on one of these boards. With each cue I said, "OK, let's go to black," so that I built the cues completely separately and there were four different looks. And these changes happened maybe two bars apart from each other. So I said, "OK, one, two, three, four." And then back to the master cue. He was astounded. And in a funny way so was I. Because even though the theory was there, I had never actually tried something like that. Then of course you had to make it so that everything was warmed up; so it worked seamlessly from one to the other.

LE TO JEFF DAVIS: *Do you recall your first experience with memory-controlled lighting? What it was, when it was?*

JEFF DAVIS: I think it was a Broadway show called *Strangers*. I certainly did find it on Broadway before I did in regional theatre. So I think it was a Broadway show that was in late '78, '79. It was a Kliegl . . . I forget what it was. It was a big black thing. It was before the Performer boards came out. I think it was the Kliegl board that came before the Performer board.

LE: *Perhaps the "Performance."*

DAVIS: I think that's what it was. It was interesting, because everyone was looking at it. It seemed like everyone sort of played on it to a certain extent. I think I was lucky in the fact that my college training was on a preset board and then I had to do piano boards. But once I realized that the Kliegl thing thought like a preset board, it wasn't very difficult for me, actually. And of course in those days all they could do was remember cues. They didn't do all the spiffy things that the boards do now. So it wasn't a matter of having to learn how things would look in different parts and how follows worked and all that other stuff. And I even think that for the first few times, I would still lay shows out as if they were on piano boards, because I had been on that logic for eight years. It took me a while to really realize I didn't have to do that just because it was the way I was used to thinking when I designed. Then after a while when I got into Light Palette and tracking I said to myself, "Oh, I can lay this out so it's memorable on the screen." It didn't matter how it was laid out to anybody else.

I think the preset way of thinking is harder to understand, but it depends on the show. If you're doing something like *Jesus Christ Superstar*, or some show where every look was a different thing, then I think that eventually the cue-only concept works better. But if you're doing a show that's a musical that's based on one idea, chances are you want cues to track, because otherwise it becomes just a high-maintenance bookkeeping problem. One of the things I said when I was advising on the Obsession makeover was that the boards had to be able to switch off tracking to do what you wanted it to do. Because some people just don't understand tracking. People who are preset-board functional don't understand tracking. I find that, from talking to people— electricians and shops and whatnot—that the only people who really understand tracking well are people that actually had to run shows on piano boards. If people didn't have that experience where the dimmer basically stayed where it was until you told it to do something else . . . apparently a lot of people have trouble with it.

Tharon was very instrumental in the Light Palette, in terms of getting it to think like a piano board, because that's what everyone on Broadway knew. I think a lot of people on Broadway were having a really hard time figuring out the cue-only process. . . . There's too much brainwork involved in it. If you want to make a change and you want it to go through seventeen cues, it's so labor-intensive.

LE TO NEIL PETER JAMPOLIS: *Do you recall the first time you used a Light Palette, a tracking-style console?*

JAMPOLIS: Yes. . . . It got away from me. What's amazing of course is that the logic of it was the logic that one was actually used to from running manual boards. . . . Somehow, it was very hard for me to make the jump, the conceptual jump, into thinking of a machine doing that and keeping track of it the same way. So I would record cues cue-only and keep going and then wonder why, when I then recorded something to track, it would stop dead after one cue and not be able to go through because there was a hard page somewhere. I wouldn't say it took all that long, maybe just one show, until the light bulb went on over my head and I thought, "Well, this is easy." In general, I have to say, for someone of my vintage as a designer, that a lot of the clarity has been due to my assistants, who would appear at various stages where this technology was either all they knew, or what they learned or so current with them that it didn't represent a change, but merely a method. They would be very patient and say, "No, no, you don't understand; you see, you just do this." And so I would rely on them to keep me up to speed. . . . Of course, it didn't take me very long to understand them, but the first time through, I think if I didn't have somebody younger or fresher to guide me through it, it probably would have been slow going.

Working on a Palette up here in Canada, the electrician automatically set the board to cue-only, and I said, "No, set it to track," which made him all nervous. He said, "Really? You can control the amount of fade and stuff?" And I said, "I'd prefer it." And he said, "Nobody I've ever worked with ever dared put it on track; they get screwed up too easily." Perhaps it's the way you started thinking. It's all fades. They saw a fade, they think you're going to wind up in a blackout. But there is such a thing as a blocking cue to take care of that problem.

LE: *Can you recall any amusing anecdotes about those early computer days?*

JAMPOLIS: Most of the amusing stories come from the old days—from the manual days, where you'd go backstage and find people in their underwear between the boards with strings in their teeth, and up around their knees and elbows, trying to execute some cue that looked effortless from the front. When we had to set up a show on road boards—I was thinking about this the other day when I was teaching—the first of my [Tony] nominations was a five-board, manually run show, *Sherlock Holmes* (and I won the Tony). You had to think of the look that you wanted, and then do the hookup so that the look could be achieved. Because if the guys couldn't grab the handles in the right places, you'd never get the look. So you really had to close your eyes and imagine the lighted stage, and then work backward and figure out where all those handles were. And it was a very physical thing. It was almost as physical for the designer, working that out. And remember, we used to do it on spreadsheets that you would draw out physically like a board in their arrangements of dimmers, and then think of the cue and look at what was involved in pulling those handles, and getting the cue to look that way. Therefore, you would have your blue-stage board, and your clear board, and your warms and your pinks, and . . . things like that. It was a whole different way of thinking, and . . . in a way there was a transition period I spoke of, where lighting wasn't very good from anybody, for a while, and then it got back on track.

WEISS: There were a dozen or so fabulous road board operators who could give you consistency. Don Stern, now owner of Bash,[18] was one of the best road board operators. I used to try to design cues that he couldn't run, but I couldn't do it. Replacement of an operator who was sick or needed some time off was always a problem because you might get a guy who had seen the show once and maybe had one rehearsal.

JAMPOLIS: I will say that what made my shows difficult to run, my manual shows—and they were—was that my cues never stopped. Among electricians, various designers had reputations for various things. If mine was anything, it was that by the time you finished with the nineteenth part of one of my cues, there was another cue running. I've carried that over into the computer control in which the cue number as recorded is just the blueprint, and then the parts go in. If I could have every lamp moving at a different speed to get the picture I want, then I would do it. They call me the "King of Parts." And then the way I write them, it always seems to be a revelation to the operator. But of course nowadays the operators are getting younger and younger. If you speak Palette, or you speak Expression, or one of those syntaxes, and you start subdividing the cue you've just written into parts, parts are the last thing that people with those boards go near. That's the hardest part to understand.

---

18. Bash was subsequently bought by Production Resource Group/Fourth Phase where Don Stern heads the lighting division.

But I am just very relaxed about it, and say, "OK, create this part, now this and this and this, and execute, and record that in part six times three, delay slash eight." And they think, "What the hell is he doing?" But it's all trying to get that look of light that never comes to rest but is always dynamic and poetic and all the things that I want light to be.

REISMAN: I'm trying to remember when I first got to use a Strand Light Palette. I did an opera at the Brooklyn Academy of Music for what was an opera company that was there for a while. It ran about two to three years and we were in the small house, not the big house. The big house had gotten the first Light Palette, or one of the first Light Palettes that fall. We went in to do this opera and they had just installed their Light Palette, and there really wasn't anybody on staff who really knew how to use the thing, and they were remodeling the dressing rooms at the same time, so all the power got interfered with. I remember trying to focus with all the lights blinking. I would say "Next," and they would say "Which one?" There would be ten lights blinking and you couldn't know which one. But that was when things really hadn't been cleaned up and that would have been because of a power problem in the building at that point. But the board had literally been installed that week and not checked out.

PARICHY: After *The Water Engine*, the first time I actually had an opportunity to use a memory board was probably a year later when I went to L.A. to do *Talley's Folly* and *Fifth of July*. Maybe it was two years later, because they had installed an early, first version of the Light Palette. I had never seen it, no one had, no one in the theatre had ever used it. We had to figure out "How the hell do we do these cues on this board? What does that mean? How can we write these cues in long ten-minute, twelve-minute fades? How do we make part cues?" No one, none of us, really knew how to do that at that point. The board was there when I arrived, and none of us had any preparation for it.

There was a period when I went with some odd boards, ones where you're trying to cope with some peculiar feature of it. One of the things I remember encountering, and there are still some boards around that have this feature . . . there was an early Century board the name of which escapes me now. It was still around just after the Palette had come out, and I was doing a show about the Beatles, or John Lennon, and it had hundreds of light cues in it, and I wanted a Light Palette, but somehow we couldn't get the Light Palette, so we took this other board. Basically what it was was a kind of two-scene preset board with a disk to record the presets. We got to the point where in the middle of the first act we discovered that it had run out of memory for the cues, and we had to figure out how the hell to switch to a different disk. No one had ever done that on that board before, and it took four disks eventually to do the show, so you had to reload the show in the middle of an act. Also, it was the only one that's ever really crashed on me during previews. I had been pretty lucky with that, and this one crashed around the fourth preview. We had to improvise how to run everything. With this kind of board, we had no kind of backup on it, and so I had to write presets, because it really had a two-scene preset part to it. Very odd.

LE: *I went through an almost year-long period myself during which I was doing a lot of assistant work, and on almost every show the board crashed. I remember it well because it was my trial as an assistant to read the show into the board off of the paper track sheets every time we would come into a theatre.*

PARICHY: I do remember a lot of problems with the Mini-Light Palette. I remember I was doing *Crimes of the Heart,* and every night during previews we had to replace the one that we had with another one.

DAVIS: One amusing story is about when I first went to Indiana Rep. They had built a new facility with two Light Palettes, one in each theatre. Prior to this, I had given the road company of *Annie* a Pong game. This was the era when they first started doing video monitors with the camera on the rail, and they had a monitor that showed programs back to the lightboard operator. They were complaining how they didn't really want to watch *Annie* all the time, for two or three years. So, for an opening night present I gave them—this was high-tech then—a Pong game. This was the high-tech computer game, right? So I gave them one and they could interface it into the monitor, backstage. When I told this story to the electrician at Indiana Rep he was very jealous that he didn't have one, and he thought it was very amusing. So I went out there, maybe four or five shows into the season, and we were doing this play that was not very cue-intensive; we would sit there for twenty-five minutes and not do any lighting, and the monitors are sitting right on the desk, so he said to me, "Reach under the table." There was a little box. I said, "OK, found it," and it was one of the controllers for a Pong game. He had the other controller up in the booth. So, suddenly . . . the Light Palette monitor would flip over to the Pong game. And it would do it on his monitor too. So we could sit there and play Pong, because we were bored. And so then I would say, "Working on cue 12" every time someone came up, like the director, to the tech room. I would say, "Working on cue 14," and the thing would flip back to Light Palette.

BILL WARFEL: I was teaching at Yale through that whole period of time, and Yale Repertory Theatre was not a wealthy theatre. We didn't have one of those boards until later than most people got them. My first design with one was Athol Fugard's play *The Road to Mecca*, which was world-premiered at Yale. And that was in '84. So that was the first time I actually used one. We had been given one by Theatre Techniques. It was a Wizard. It was built in Israel and it was not a reliable piece of equipment. Theatre Techniques tried several times to fix it. They eventually gave us a new one, and even yet it never, never came around. So, my first experience was with the opening night crowd, with the critics and everybody there, and at the beginning of Act Two it started a slow fade to blackout which would not be reversed: "Thank you very much, I'm going out." And we ran the show manually. Fortunately, that board had manual sliders. That was the only way we managed to get through the rest of the evening. So that is where I was with respect to memory boards during this specific period of time that you're talking about. I was a great supporter of them. I was a great believer that they were eventually going to become extremely reliable and the way to go, and that they would be a great liberating factor. I preached this sermon in my classes; I went to every manufacturer's "here's our latest memory board" rollout. I collected stories of nightmares not unlike the one that I just described to you. There was a lot going on and I was happy to be waiting for it to break over my head. And when it did, that's exactly what it did do. At any rate, that's where I was with it.

■

The Strand Light Palette dominated the commercial market in the 1980s and into the 1990s. The Kliegl Performer was another popular console in the 1980s. By the mid 1990s, Strand's sales in the U.S. were surpassed by ETC, maker of the Expression, a highest-takes-precedence console, and the Obsession, a last-action console similar in functionality to the Light Palette.

LE TO FRED FOSTER: *Is it true that you built the very first console with your brother Bill on a dare from Gilbert Hemsley?*

FRED FOSTER: As I remember the story, I took Bill down to look at the Q-File [at UW–Madison Department of Theatre and Drama] and his direct quote was, "Gack! We can do this for $5,000." So we thought about it, and then Christmas Eve of 1975 we went over to Gilbert's house, to one of his parties, and got an audience with him. That meant you went to some place that was a little bit quieter than some of the other places in the house, and whoever was interested came along. So we ended up in Gilbert's bedroom. David Thurow was there, Alan Adelman was there; whoever happened to be there at the time was sitting around on whatever they could find to sit on. We said, "We're going to make a Q-File." And everybody said, "Yeah, sure. Yeah, whatever you think." And they basically dismissed it—dismissed the concept of it. We just felt challenged by that—or at least not disheartened—and decided to go off and do it.

In the course of time, Gilbert said that he would try to get Joel Rubin to buy it at Kliegl. We actually thought we were going to a USITT conference on Kliegl's nickel with a prototype to sell it to Kliegl, but by then they had Gordon [Pearlman]'s Performance board. So I don't know if it was just because Gilbert dared us to do it. It was probably because everybody said we couldn't do it that spurred us on. We just decided this was something we wanted to do. Like when we were still in high school, we talked about making preset boards.

LE: *And is your brother still involved, or . . . ?*

FOSTER: He's kind of a consultant, but no, he isn't really involved. He's a physicist down at Fermi Lab. I think initially there wasn't much art in what computerized lighting consoles were. Certainly that's true of the group of us developing the first console, my brother and myself—my knowledge of lighting and the demands of it were so small. Our first work was really just duplicating Q-File with a microprocessor and adding a few things to it, such as having a CRT display as part of it; there was obviously a lot more information you could combine. The enhancements that we made to it weren't just technological enhancements. They would come from discussions where I would be wiring a circuit and my brother would be programming something, and I would hear him say, "Fred, how gross would it be if ___?" And these would range from "How gross would it be if when I record a cue, a fade stops until it writes to disk?"—which would obviously be *too* gross—to "How gross would it be if instead of displaying just all the information in a single cue, you displayed the level of one channel in all of the cues and then you could do range changes?" Which was the inception of the concept of track sheets, although it was a kind of one-dimensional track sheet. Those enhancements were interesting because they didn't come out of a traditional marketing model where you say, here's a market need for something, or the competition does it, so we have to do it. It came out of the programmer looking at it, an engineer looking at a data structure and saying, "You know, it's just as easy to split the data up this way as it is that way." And that turned out to be a really useful tool. There were ideas that we had then—just to carry that thought along—to display one channel in bar graphs. (This has been done subsequently by other manufacturers.) We looked at that and suggested it to lighting designers and said, "Would it be useful for us to show you channel information this way, with a fader that would let you select all these channels and proportionally raise and lower them and then you can see it graphically?" And the answer would be, "No, that's not going to be useful, because I don't think that way; it would be in the way, it wouldn't be efficient." It wasn't really until we had a working prototype and had any penetration into the market that we had feedback; it took us a long time to get to that point.

LE: *When was this?*

FOSTER: Well, Christmas Eve of '75 was when we started the original product, and we had the first working product Christmas of '76, which we used for the first time in '77. Then we took it to a trade show and sold it to manufacturers. It took us until USITT in 1978 to actually have a product that could be shown in front of the customers as a product. That was the Channel Track for Colortran. Although Colortran gave us some feedback on how it should work, it wasn't really until then that customers, end users, started to see how the product worked. And even through the days of Colortran, we didn't, as the developers of the system, have significant contact with the end user. So we weren't getting any feedback. What little feedback we would get would be filtered through Colortran's marketing department. And it really wasn't very substantial. So a lot of what we did was really the result of my guessing what would be a useful tool, designing the product, and then some neat little ideas and other stuff would crop into it.

The first time that I recall having substantial feedback on what the system should do from an end user was when we started working with John Haupt at Disney to develop a lighting system for Epcot. That would have been 1980 that we started working on that. He had a functional specification that didn't say too much about the operation of it. But then we really started thinking more about what features we could add, what other products were in the marketplace, what Light Palette, Performer, the other competitive products were doing, and as such we . . . boy, I haven't thought about this for a long time . . . I think we did a lot more. There were endless discussions that were really internal discussions, about how cross-fades should work, how tracking should work. What really happens when you record a cue here, how far should it track, how do you warn people. I remember one of the big discussions when we started putting "track and record" into what was essentially a preset board, or Performer-style operation, was a concern I had heard expressed at trade shows by people not familiar with Light Palette, that you change one cue and all of a sudden cue 55 is much different. And that was one of the early paranoias about a tracking-style console. So we came up with something that has now devolved out of our consoles, which was a mini track sheet, which when you selected a channel it would show you five cues before and five cues after the cue you were editing. And if you were going to do a "track and record" with it you could see a trail of where it was going as a warning device, which actually is something we should consider throwing back in our console, because it's quite useful. One of the thoughts on it is "I want to know how I got to it." I'm editing this channel, in this cue, but "where was it before?" and "where is it going to go?" is useful information to have. Still, most of the time it was what we thought would be a neat feature, and it was pretty insular.

LE: *When did you stop being involved with Colortran?*

FOSTER: We did Channel Track from 1978 through 1981. Then we did the Patchman console for them in about 1983 and then by '84 or '85 we were fundamentally done with our deal with them. We started selling product under our own name in 1982, to Disney, when we delivered the first of the ELC [Entertainment Lighting Controllers] consoles to Disney. Then we launched ETC-branded products at the USITT conference in 1983 at Corpus Christi. So that was really the first time that we were starting to sell directly. We offered the product to Colortran, but they were tired of dealing with these flakes from Wisconsin who would rather be sailing, and we were tired of dealing with them, so we just split ways at that point.

LE: *What console was that in '83?*

FOSTER: It was the first of the Concept consoles. It was an outgrowth of the work we did for Epcot, the Entertainment Lighting Controllers that we did for Disney. I can remember having a Concept console, which had 125 control channels and two screens and twenty-four submasters, which is really the physical embodiment of the entire Expression line of products, which is descended from this product. Some things like the number of submasters have changed. If I had designed a lightboard, I would never have had any manual faders on it. In fact, our original prototype had no sliders on it whatsoever. John Haupt said, "We need twenty-four submasters." He had asked Kliegl and Strand at the time if they would do a board to this spec, and they said "No." So our willingness to do it was how we ended up getting that contract. We took that input, which did counter what I thought, because I had basically come out of the Q-File concept with prethought cues and do-everything-as-a-move rather than any kind of dynamic control of lighting.

We had this product and developed a way of trying to distribute it. We were making the control consoles and going to Strand and Colortran and Kliegl and Electro Controls—at the time all full-range manufacturers. That forced us into a business structure where we teamed up with Teatronics and Lighting Methods, who just did dimmers and couldn't afford to do consoles. So that product at that point was about competitive to where the Performer was, which was selling for about $30,000. The Performer had really carved out the professional off-Broadway and Broadway touring market. The Performer II was, probably, the more successful of the two.

We tried to figure out how we were going to get our product into the professional market. We went through Lighting Methods. I remember taking one of the early Concepts down to Production Arts, with Lighting Methods, and Steve Terry had Ken Billington and Jason Kantrowitz come over and look at it. And, oh, they just shredded it. My favorite comment, which I still like to tease Jason about, is that when he looked at the touch faders on it he said, "Well, couldn't you have made those pink and green, rather than this blue?" Here I was looking for some kind of valid feedback on how to make the product better and I got color comments.

At that point we started running into problems. What we had was a product that was essentially equivalent to Performer, but we weren't Kliegl, we didn't have the market niche. Susan . . . Titus—now Susan Foster—was working for us, and she took the face panel layout of the Concept, which was quite wide, with twenty-four submasters, two time faders, and the keyboard, and cut out all the control surfaces, and on a sheet of paper this big did what became the Idea console, the original Idea console, which had twelve submasters, one time fader, and the keypad section, and was something only this big. She said, "This is what you should make." Or, "This is what we should make." And then we looked at it and said, "Hey, that's a pretty good idea." And you can lay that paste-up drawing down on the face panel of the machine we eventually made, and that's essentially it. Now the product can sell for $10,000 rather than $25,000 or $30,000. We came back at Steve Terry again and he was resistant, and I finally said in frustration, "Steve, tell me what I have to do to get you to buy some of these." And he said, "Sell me five of them

for $5,000 apiece." And I said, "OK, I will." And I could hear him say
"Fuck!" over the phone. So at that point he started selling these, and he
was making good money off them, because he could rent them out close
to the price he could rent out a five-scene preset and be unique to the
market niche. This was when we started getting a lot more feedback from
the marketplace, because now our products were being used by lighting
designers who care. It's probably safe to say that anyone who ended up
with an early ETC console from either Lighting Methods or Teatronics
at that time wanted a Kliegl product or wanted a Strand product, but
they got us. And so all of a sudden we had people giving Steve Terry a lot
of feedback, which would percolate back to us.

I asked Steve Terry about the feedback he was receiving on some of
the boards he was renting out during this period.

TERRY: I had a lot of input on the Performer, less on Performance,
because Production Arts wasn't in the memory system business until
Performer showed up. We were the first customer for five Performer I
consoles.

LE: *I rented some from you.*

TERRY: Yeah, did they work?

LE: *We got stuck a few times.*

TERRY: The early Performer I was a really nasty console.

LE: *I remember having to set the little dipswitches so I could have backup
every time we needed it. This would be around 1985.*

TERRY: That would be Performer II. We got LMI [Lighting Methods,
Inc.] to build an output card for the Performer II that spit out Micro II
protocol to drive the high-density racks that we had commissioned from
LMI.[19] Basically, they designed the dimmer and we designed the racks.
We had this protocol, this was before DMX, and we had to make the
Performer II drive them, so we reverse engineered the Performer II to

---

19. Micro II was LMI's proprietary protocol at that time.

give it digital output. That had little dipswitches on it too. You had to get the number of panels just right . . . it was really convoluted.

We sent out a lot of tours with that system. We were really scared about the cable, the idea of putting all those dimmers on one multiplex cable. We had an A cable and a B cable and a status cable so that you could switch between them. We were definitely worried about the idea of a multiplex protocol and its reliability. Somewhat unfounded fears, but . . . you certainly had all your eggs in one basket, on that one cable, and there wasn't any really durable portable cable like there is now. It was kind of normal data cable that belonged in a conduit, not lying on the floor.

DAVIS: The Expression board still baffles me, partially because I think it has much too many buttons to push. I never could understand: record it, load it here, then it goes into a screen and it disappears off the screen and you go, "Where'd that go?" But I know I'm in the minority, because it's probably the most popular board out there. It's just that my thinking isn't preset-oriented.

■

LE TO CURT OSTERMANN: *When we spoke last you said I should ask you about the board at Radio City Music Hall.*[20]

OSTERMANN: In the 1930s when that board was designed, it was the first time the dimmers and the controls were in separate places in any theatre in America, maybe in the world. It was probably the first time they had the lighting control in front of house. At Radio City it just happens to be a little appendage to the orchestra pit. The lightboard is just downstage of the conductor.

LE: *Still?*

OSTERMANN: Oh, yes, definitely. And it was thyratron reactor dimmers in a big room with either a five-scene or ten-scene preset—I think it was a ten-scene preset. The grand masters, or grand faders, were crank-types that go in circles, with little handles. So to crank a cue up on a bump

---

20. After this interview, the architectural and stage lighting at Radio City Music Hall was significantly updated, and the thyratron tube dimmers were replaced by digital dimmers.

you gotta turn the handle as fast as you can for three or four seconds. Because back then in the '30s, everything was thought of as radio dials, nothing had turned into linear control, yet. But I have worked at Radio City recently and there is still all this stuff that is hard-wired. All the cove lighting in the ceiling, the built-in footlights, all of the architectural lighting details, those are hard-wired to the old boards. So if you want to use that stuff—and you would never go into Radio City and not use that stuff—you use the original board to control that, and then we usually have an Obsession down there to control all of the modern lighting, the stage lighting. Every time I work there it's a little bit of both. It's an Obsession controlling most of the stage stuff and that wonderful ten-scene preset down there from the '30s, or maybe even 1929.

LE: *Are they still driving thyratron tube dimmers?*

OSTERMANN: Yes. I think it's GE that still makes . . .

LE: *Those purple tubes.*

OSTERMANN: I've been in that room. I remember when Rich Claffey, the head electrician there, took me into the dimmer room a couple of years ago to look at them. It's very, very much like *The Wizard of Oz*. Wonderful. And it still works. But you know that was, my God, that was early, and having the front end separated from the dimmers was a big deal, and I remember that's the one huge thing that happened on Broadway. When computer control happened, all of a sudden the electricians could see their work. That was the first time ever. Before, they were either in the basement, in the fly floor, or backstage controlling the lighting, and they never saw the result of their work. And when computers came on, they could go front of house, with the front end of the console, and start watching everything. And on *Chorus Line* it was critical that the bump cues happen in the right place. So with the stage manager and the electrician out front of house, it was just a much cleaner show. So that was a huge change—I forgot about that—getting the lighting personnel out front of house. But the producers hated it, because to accommodate the electrician and the console, they had to lose seats.

SECTION 2

Vari-Lite and the Prevalence of Automation

Once computerized lighting control became the norm, the way was paved for other electronic developments, including remotely controlled (automated) moving lights. Before there were fully automated moving lights, there were automated color-changing devices on the market, including indexing color wheels and semaphore-style color changers. Vari-Lites, specifically the VL2 series, become the moving light of choice for concert venues throughout the 1980s. By the mid 1990s, Vari-Lites, as well as automated lights manufactured by High End, Morpheus, and, to a lesser degree, Clay Paky and Martin, were used in the design of more traditional theatrical performances from Broadway to not-for-profit resident theatres, and to colleges and universities. I asked designers about their first experiences with automated lights and Tom Littrell of Vari-Lite about his recollections of the development of the very first Vari-Lite, the VL1.

KEN BILLINGTON: I remember that when we used to use semaphore color changers I had a separate console for them and even before that, Lycian used to make an indexing color wheel. I would have my six colors in a color wheel, but you had to preset them all and it was a separate panel for control and pushing buttons and a prayer, "Please, let's hope they move." But it was great. I used to use those old indexing color wheels in the '70s—if I could get a shop to buy them. Now the shops will buy you the stuff.

TOM LITTRELL: Showco's first idea was to have a color-changing PAR. Jim Bornhorst had an idea to switch from a semaphore-style changer to something more integral to the unit. Jack Maxson suggested it not only change color, but move as well.[1]

> Vari-Lite, as a company, grew out of Showco and introduced their first fixtures on the 1981 Genesis tour in Barcelona, Spain. Alan Owen was the designer and Tom Littrell was the programmer.

LE: *What was Alan Owen's relationship to Showco?*

LITTRELL: He was an employee of Showco; freelance designers were a lot less common. If you hired a lighting company, you got the designer that came along with it, or your favorite designer was within the ranks of your favorite company; that was a far more common way to do business at that time, in the '70s.

So much has changed. [The concert industry] resembles theatrical lighting more now in that there are designers and there are vendors, and everybody comes together in the guise of a specific project.

LE: *What was the design application for that first Vari-Lite fixture? What were you and Alan Owen and Genesis really going for with that first fixture? What were you trying to achieve with it?*

LITTRELL: We did not have many preconceptions about what we really wanted in it. The most exciting thing to me, still to this day, is lighting that is music-motivated lighting . . . to me it's the greatest combination of the kind of art that a painter does and the kind of art that a theatrical designer does, where there are requirements to illuminate the stage, but there aren't as many design constraints as there are when you're doing a straight play or even a musical; you can open up a lot more. You can really walk into a situation without any "malice of forethought." You walk into a situation, hear the music, see what the band is doing on stage, and paint with light on top of that. Good [concert] design does go back to the same principles that a theatre designer goes for. You have to illuminate the stage, you have to draw focus to this area or that, but it can be a lot more arbitrary in terms of color and angles or however you decide to emphasize the moment. Then on top of that you have the

---

1. Jim Bornhorst of Showco led the engineering team that developed the VL1 moving light. Jack Maxson remains one of the principal owners of Vari-Lite, Inc.

musical moments. We walked in just knowing that these lights would be an excellent tool to help paint pictures that we wanted to paint on a Genesis stage.

LE: *You've talked in previous interviews about the idea of all the lights being choreographed in unison and how strong that idea was. Did you also use them as individual fixtures? The reason I'm asking this question is because that's how they're predominantly used now in theatrical applications.*

LITTRELL: Actually, the idea of a color-changing, reprogrammable, repositionable spot luminaire came first; that was the original goal. We thought about this as theatre designers. We wanted to be able to use a light stage right as a downlight over a stage right position, or a pipe end cross-stage light for a stage left position across the stage, and then also be able to change colors. This is a point that Rusty [Brutsche, president of Vari-Lite] often makes. It was only after we hung the first few lights that we got working in a row in the shop, and addressed them all as one and started moving them in unison that we realized the power that that kind of movement could have. We may or may not have known it consciously, but it was only after we saw it that we realized that that was the big selling point in the early days: the notion of choreographed movement as a design element rather than just something you did in the dark to get from point A to point B. So many of the wonderful cues that we did in those days were literally by accident. You programmed a look . . . say cue 11 and then you programmed cue 12, and then, when you executed the cues, you realized that the movement getting there was more stunning than either of the static looks.

LE: *Actually seeing the fixtures move was an important part of it?*

LITTRELL: Right. And that goes along with the whole notion of music . . . the idea of the lighting being a kind of a painting on top of the music, reflecting the music. The music moves, and then so do the lights. And one of the impetuses to building a system like Vari-Lite was the fact that designers had attempted to get that type of movement before, but it was with more and more and more PAR cans. By the late '70s, there were rigs—like on the Van Halen tour—with a thousand PAR cans.

LE: *Can you describe your experience on that first Genesis tour?*

LITTRELL: With Genesis you had amazingly theatrical music and just free rein to do the most incredible arbitrary lighting cues you could come up with, and a really wonderful design process because it was really design by committee at its best. It was Alan [Owen] and the band sitting on the sidelines and I was there pushing buttons. Alan had worked for the band for several years prior to that and had a great rapport with them. We would literally rent department store dummies, mannequins, and put them on stage after they were finished with rehearsals, and we would sit back in the back of the room and run cues. And we would come up with these, dare I say it, splendid looks, and the band would say, "That's really an excellent look, but we really feel that as being more part of that song rather than this song," and they would have these really nice insights about how they felt about the music. We'd write these tremendous cues, and they'd say, "That's fantastic, but don't use it here, use it there." And we would change things around that way. Or . . . a lot of times they would simplify for us, because we would want to get really ditsy with our cuing—almost prissy.

To get back to this notion of unison, it's amazing what 150 lights all in red does to a stage coming out of a cue with different lights and different angles and different colors. We would try to go from one multicolor look to another, but the band would say, "Wait a minute—don't—we like the first look, but come out of that into just a solid red stage." Which we had avoided doing because it seemed too easy: just one button and it was all there. But then when we ran it, it worked. It was stunning to go from a little of this and a little of that to a lot of one thing. That's one of the things that Vari-Lites could give you: just the red light wasn't just another group of lights with red gels. The red light came from every single light on stage. And that kind of simplicity—and the same goes for movement— was intense. This idea of movement in unison versus not in unison: You can get these stunning looks with every light doing different things, kind of the ballyhoo from hell, or every single light can start upstage and sweep downstage, through the audience and up into the truss, which is something that's the easiest cue in the world to program, but in the right time and the right place it's a drop-dead cue. So that was Genesis.

LE: *What was the controller at that time? You had not yet developed the Artisan, is that right?*

<u>LITTRELL:</u> Right. The Artisan didn't come along until 1986. There was a one-of-a-kind controller built that was a 32-channel controller that stored 255 cues that we built for the very first Genesis tour, the 1981 tour that started in Barcelona. In 1982 we built the Series 100 controller that worked then for the next several years, which would control up to 96 instruments but it would store only 239 cues. . . . By today's standards they were very very crude. On the other hand, they established a lot of the ways of controlling moving lights that are still present on our consoles and in other moving light consoles to this day: a whole different way of thinking about talking to lights, rather than a pan fader, a tilt fader, an intensity fader. Rather than thinking in terms of how to make a regular lighting console or a normal lighting console control moving lights, we started from scratch and built a console to control the lights.

<u>LE:</u> *What kind of features did that first controller have? How did it interface between the designer and the lights?*

<u>LITTRELL:</u> What it did was what a good moving light controller still does, and that is, once a light was selected, there were multiple knobs and faders which allowed you to address the different attributes simultaneously and at any time, without having to select and deselect channels as you did that. One of the problems with a conventional console, although a lot of the consoles now are building in features that make this possible, was that once you had moved pan where you wanted the light to pan, then you had to deselect the pan channel and then go into the tilt channel and then tilt the light down, and you realized your pan was slightly off once you got the tilt about right, and that back and forth is agonizing if you're trying to program a whole lot of lights. Brooks Taylor was the software designer behind the way we started controlling moving lights. He conceived of a communication process where you selected the light, which just opened the door to communication, and then you just started turning the knobs as fast as you could to get where you wanted it.

I've always thought of it as being like a good typist; you can do different things with different fingers almost at the same time. I mean, a good moving light programmer is moving pan and tilt at the same time, and his pinkie is reaching up to tap the color button at the same time. But you tell a good typist they have to push one letter at a time with a mouse, and they'll just look at you crazed—but that is a lot of the time just what programming moving lights with conventional consoles feels like. That was the main thing about that first console that's still in use today. And there are a lot of other subtle philosophical things. It's strictly a snapshot console, for example. You made the stage look like you wanted it and you pushed the store button and that was the cue, period, the end. That was an important thing when you're dealing with moving lights. The other very important thing was the notion that if a light had no intensity, it stored nothing, so it would sit where you last left it. A lot people, when they first started trying to deal with moving lights, thought that was a weakness, but the more you deal with them, the more you realize that's a strength. You don't want a light that's sitting there off moving around based on where it happened to be when you stored that cue. That really does open up the door to a lot of scary things when every light stores its position regardless of whether or not it's on. Or we thought so and still believe that.

LE: *Once the 100 series was introduced, did Vari-Lite solicit input from designers on the design of subsequent fixtures? How much back and forth was there between Vari-Lite and the people who use them?*

LITTRELL: There was a lot of input. There was a lot of training and learning going on both from our point of view and the designers' point of view. There were really designers on the vanguard like Alan Owen and Allen Branton and . . . Roy Bennett. I hate to name names because I know I'm going to leave somebody out . . . but those folks were really the ones who got it. . . . They got the first lights.

ALLEN BRANTON: In 1982, I had been doing the lighting for the Diana Ross show for about three years. We had a method of lighting the band in down pools, using 6 X 16 lekos. When the Vari-Lite became available, Vari-Lite let us use them in Las Vegas on a trial basis, to see if she would enjoy them. Basically, I took the lekos down and put the Vari-Lites in that slot to start. These were the VL1, which was a kind of very crude automated hard-edged light. Compared to the lights today, it was a very crude, very unreliable light—a mess. At the time, though, it seemed like a miracle. I think we had eighteen lights in that first package. We put those lights up in the overhead or in our lighting rig, depending if we were in a theatre or on a tour with trusses. There was a down special or steep back on each band member, of which there were twelve or fourteen if I recall. And so instead of having a leko over each one and three colors, I had this apparatus over each one and virtually unlimited colors.

LE: *Was color changing the most important feature for you?*

BRANTON: Well, who knew? We were just starting. It gave me a lot of variety in the way the show could look. That was a pretty simple, modestly budgeted production, with Diana Ross just doing her cabaret act with a fourteen- or fifteen-piece band and some simple scenery and platforms and some soft goods, backgrounds and such. There were general washes, front and back, and low side washes, and I used gel changers on those side washes, so that between that and the overhead Vari-Lites there was a hell of a lot of potential color variation. I'm just remembering this as I talk about it, but another significant factor was that all the scenery was white and her band all dressed in white, and so the color variation was quite dramatic compared to a more normal arrangement with darker colors in clothing and scenery. That's where I started with it. I figured overhead was a very safe place to put these because I know they will do what I've been doing from that position and get me back to where I was very very quickly; then I could build from there. You must understand there was no rehearsal or any preparation to speak of. We would load into Las Vegas and virtually do the show the same night. That is why I had to start from a place that was fairly conservative so I could get back, at least, to a show that I had been doing and then, as I said, build from there. Las Vegas was a great place to be, by the way, because once you're set up, you're there for two or three weeks and you have two shows a night, and you can put in a few new things at virtually every show, and the look of the show makes quite a bit of progress in that two- or three-week period. You're basically developing it with a live audience.

Eventually, we added some stunts and moving effects and things like that—all the things that Genesis had done up to that time. I think only Genesis and ZZ Top had had these lights prior to us, and those had been with in-house Vari-Lite designers. There just was not a hell of a lot of doctrine about what you do with this stuff. Nobody had had a chance to do it. Tom Littrell was my operator and he had been out on Genesis, so he had a body of experience that he could pull from and from which he could offer me ideas. He would say, "Well, we can try this; we can try that; we can try this other thing; it can do this, it does that; this is interesting." We started by adapting some of those Genesis thoughts to Diana's music and her show. And then in time I had my own ideas once I got comfortable with what the parameters of the technology were. Again, probably a lot more than the layman realizes, the logistics of the show you're doing have an effect. That is, where is it going to go? How much time are you going to have to prepare it if you want to change something or try something new? (Particularly if it's fairly radical, like taking those sixteen lights down and putting them somewhere else next week.) It's very hard to do that because you don't have any time to prepare or test. The lights don't just do these things all by themselves, as you know. So it . . . builds fairly slowly.

LE: *As you started to use Vari-Lites, or any automated fixture more, what kind of features were you looking for specifically? What did you want that you had to push them towards developing in the fixtures?*

BRANTON: I don't mean to be a pain in the ass, but I'm not sure if in those early days that premise really existed. There was so little of it, and it was such a spectacular thing, even in the state it was in, that I'm not sure we spent all that much time thinking about what it should do other than what it did. Now, having said that, we were really frustrated with the notion that there was no programmable time in it. Everything had to happen manually. There was no time on the color changes or time on the gobo changes or time on anything except the iris. It was all manual. And so we said, "Well, gosh, wouldn't it be great if we had time on this thing?" And "wouldn't it be great if you didn't have to slam all these effects in, you could dissolve them in?" and so forth. Now, to this day [May 1997], there's no hard-edged Vari-Lite, or any hard-edged light of anybody's (except maybe Morpheus had one for a while) that can dissolve color or dissolve gobos or anything like that, because by necessity they're all on a wheel, so it just doesn't really work like that. What one does is, over time, just adapt your thinking to what the thing gives you. All design is, is basically constraints, and then what you use is what's left.

LITTRELL: All of the timing was done manually. If you wanted a five-second fadeout you pulled the fader down in five seconds. It was the automated lighting equivalent of just a two-scene fader board with no timing functions. The designers and we as the programmers realized immediately that we needed timing built into this thing. We needed the ability to do a ten-second fade in intensity, but also ten-second movements. And the designers asked for that really quickly and we got that to them with the next console, with the Series 200 console.

LE: *What other features did designers ask for?*

LITTRELL: Overall, the first lights were wonderful and exciting and in a lot of ways fairly crude. They wanted and asked for more subtlety, and they started that fairly quickly. It took us a while to be able to deliver that because that's an engineering process.

LE: *By subtlety, do you mean better resolution?*

LITTRELL: Better resolution of movement and more even color distribution. The original source for the Vari-Lite was a bulb called the General Electric Marc 350, which was about the only game in town at that point. Unfortunately, you could pull ten of them out of the box brand new and get about eight different shades of white before you even started putting the color mechanism in front of them. And then the dichroic coating process had to get more and more sophisticated. If we make fifty lights in red, and a couple of them are slightly off, nobody really notices. But if you put fifty lights in the equivalent of a lux 33 pink[2] and the color is slightly off, everybody notices.

And, the designers wanted more sophistication in the lights. Actually, we were, to be really honest, we were pulled in all directions. If they were bright they wanted brighter; if they were subtle they wanted subtler. It was really like a wildfire situation: No matter what they got, the better they got at using what we gave them, the more they wanted something a little better. And that's still the case today.

BRANTON: Let me go back to Diana Ross. Eventually we came out of that cabaret setting. She was on a career resurgence trajectory at that time ('82,

---

2. Roscolux 33 is a very pale tint, called "No Color Pink."

'83, '84), so the next year, or I guess actually later that year, she went to a big worldwide arena tour. We did places like the L.A. Forum and Madison Square Garden and the like, with the stage in the center and audience in the round—big audiences: ten, fifteen, twenty thousand. So in that particular application we stopped using the Vari-Lites on the band and used them on the stage itself. Because of being in an arena, the only scenic element was a white, round disk that she would perform on, about 30 feet in diameter. We would paint it multicolors with the Vari-Lites or we would do stunts all over the arena. The Vari-Lites became a very powerful tool for this kind of tent revival drill that she does really well with audiences that large. To this day I think that's one of the more effective uses of that technology: to touch the audience with it in appropriate ways and bring that enthusiasm back to the stage and vice versa—symbolically, of course. That's totally antithetical to traditional theatre and all that, but with this raw musical variety entertainment—there's no structure, so you make it up. If the house is coming down you know you must be doing something right. It's very much a trial-and-error affair. I didn't want to leave out that "theatre in the round" idea, because that was actually quite important.

LE: *So, you used more movement for the arena shows?*

BRANTON: Yes. Typically, there were three or four elements. First of all, we had four trusses around an arena, at 12 o'clock, 6 o'clock, 3 o'clock, 9 o'clock, with colored ACLs[3] on them for color pools over the whole arena. We would use these quite often, because Diana really wanted to see the audience and she wanted to see that they saw that she could see them. And then when you would lay the moving effects or Vari-Lite stunts onto an already receptive environment, you could get some major hysteria going in the audience. In the middle of an arena, she had to run about 100 feet from the stage back to the quick-change booth, and do the ubiquitous costume change. It had to happen every fifteen minutes or so, so when she would leave the stage, we would always do lighting effects; we would do everything we could to melt the place down, to maintain visual stimulation until she got back. With a star like that, it's really interesting how incredibly plain and pathetic any environment becomes once they leave it.

---

3. An "ACL" is an aircraft landing light, a very narrow-beamed, low-voltage PAR lamp.

At times we would choreograph cues that would move specifically from her or the stage area in tune with the crowd. For example she would, at the end of the show, come to her big power ballad, which was the Lionel Ritchie song "Endless Love." At the end she would improvise on the lyrics and with her own body language take the mood into an "I'm singing to every person in the crowd" kind of vibe—and very effectively. Then, just about the time that everybody was about to burst into tears, she would say "Good night." We would do this gentle lift of all the lights, which had been on the stage in some very delicate gobo pattern or something, we would do this gentle lift of the lights up through the crowd, and with just a little bit of . . . retinal stimulation . . . and they were up on their feet. Now, they may have been anyway, but that sort of thing was really effective in terms of projecting those moods into a giant audience. The sort of intimacy that an effective concert needs is hard to get in those big toilets. But people play them because there's a lot of money, you know. The economics kind of dictate it.

Branton, with Littrell as operator, went on to use Vari-Lites in his design of the 1983 David Bowie tour.

LITTRELL: David Bowie got a lot closer to theatre lighting because of the way David's show was. David himself thought in the terms of a stage performer/director. In other words, "For this song I will be here and my musicians will be there, and we'll hit these marks and we'll build looks around this." In that sense, David's show was assembled far more like a regular theatrical performance in that David and his choreographer and his musicians and Allen at the lighting console would build scenes based on the lights and the stage performers having "malice of forethought" as far as where they're going to stand and how they wanted the scene to read. And David's show, especially for that time, had a lot of scenic elements.

LE: *His shows were more concept-oriented? They had more of a story to them?*

LITTRELL: That's it exactly. It was very much a music concert, but the songs had settings, and as he conceived of his show, each song had a different little scenic hook. At one point I recollect we built a look around David kneeling center stage and pointing outward, and the band was gathered around him and they were all looking off into the distance, and the whole notion was to create the look of one of those 1920s Russian revolutionary posters—the proletariat looks bravely into the future. The discussion was held on that level. It was really neat to be there, because they were discussing "this is how we want that to look, and we want the colors to be bright but not garish, the way those posters were big solid blocks of colors," and the format of those posters from the '20s coming out of the Soviet Union. It was very intellectual . . . and huge fun.

BRANTON: On the Bowie show, he never attempted to cut any corners on rehearsal time. He's such a perfectionist and such a smart person basically. I did two tours with him, and we always had plenty of rehearsal time and a very coherent assembly plan just in terms of the show—choreography, sound, lighting, costumes, and everything—and a proper director. That's unusual in rock shows. Depending on the artist they may give you a few days, they may give you some weeks, or someone like Michael Jackson would always take a month or so. But other artists wouldn't take any time at all. I don't do that many tours any more and that [lack of rehearsal time] is a lot of the reason that I don't. . . . I just can't do much without rehearsal and preparation. There are a lot of shortcuts to get around that and a lot of people use them, but they don't particularly work for me or interest me, and I've really been lucky to have my television work grow so much in the last several years so I haven't needed to live in that crazy world. That is a very artist-specific phenomenon. Some people are wonderful about it and others are just useless. They think you order these shows like you order a pizza.

LE: *Did you have any problems with the Vari-Lites, other than needing rehearsal time to program them?*

BRANTON: One thing that we were a bit frustrated by and we got really burned by on the Bowie tour was that in the beginning there was no disk drive or any sort of backup memory apparatus [on the Vari-Lite controller].

<u>LE:</u> *Ouch.*

<u>BRANTON:</u> Your show was in that console and that was it. There was no way to extract the show from the console and take it someplace else. There were only two or three Vari-Lite tours out at one time. This was the really, really early days; it was very primitive. I'm sure it occurred to them that they needed this someday, but it was just down the list of priorities, and it hadn't come up as a problem before.

Let me go further back. When they would go out on a Genesis tour, it would begin and they would program it, and it would run until it was done. With the same equipment package and the whole thing. There weren't enough lights to be jumping from continent to continent and trying to use duplicate equipment or anything like that. That was just not in the cards. With Diana Ross, maybe we'd come together after a break and reprogram the thing from scratch, but it was so few lights and the things you were doing were so simple that if I had an operator who was familiar with the show, we would just quickly build from scratch. (In the beginning my operator was Tom and then it was C. D. Simpson, and then Arthur Smith.) So that wasn't a big problem. But then we go to David Bowie. We program him in Dallas, in the spring of '83. Then we have a couple of weeks' break and we're expected to turn up in Brussels and dust this whole thing off and open the show there. It was a couple of days before the actual opening and so we do more programming and so on—that all goes beautifully and everybody's delighted. That was one of the most satisfying shows I've ever done. The most satisfying, in terms of rock concert work. But we have this sort of ugly problem looming. He, Bowie, has agreed to play at the US Festival in California about ten days hence. We were worried about the fact that we had to cover that show with duplicate equipment. But he's also playing his tour in Europe, and they're just going to charter a jet and fly everybody there and do the show and come back. This is the first time that Vari-Lite has ever had to try to put a show with its cues in two places at once. And there was no way to take that programming, those memories, out of that console, which was in Brussels, and take them any place else. So they think, "Well, maybe we could figure out a way to copy the information from the cue memory cards into another set of cue memory cards."

LE: *Did you have any of this on paper, in the type of track sheet format used in theatre at the time?*

BRANTON: Yes and no. We knew where and what all the cues were. We knew where they all went, and in general they were tied to the material in the show, but for example, there was a song called "Fame," a Bowie classic. There was all this ballyhoo and "bright lights, big city" kind of action: very, very busy and very wild. In effect, there was no way to record it; you could write that down as a concept, but how would you codify that information? The moves were done manually by the operator.

LE: *There wouldn't have been a way to preprogram something in the shop the way you could today?*

BRANTON: No. You could preprogram it, but you couldn't take what you'd preprogrammed any place because you had no way to carry it. There was no memory. All the work we did lived inside that one console. And there was no way to transfer that data to another console.

LE: *What ended up happening?*

BRANTON: Vari-Lite sent a guy out to Brussels, Dale Polansky. (You may have heard of him because there were four original operators that could program these lights: Tom [Littrell] and C. D. [Simpson] and Dale, and a guy named Jim Waits was the fourth.[4] Tom and C. D. and Dale went to college together (that's a very interesting story, too). Polansky comes out to Brussels with the idea that he's going to copy the information in our cue memory cards into another set of cue memory cards from the main computer. And so he attempted this little exercise right after our Brussels show. He takes off with the cards and goes back to America, and supposedly we're going to plug these into a console in California in about a week and our show will be there, we think. So lo and behold we get to Frankfurt the next day and in the process of doing this, Dale has erased all the show out of some of those cards.

LE: *I knew something like this was coming.*

---

4. Jim Waits is now Vari-Lite's head of educational outreach.

BRANTON: So everything stage left of center (this is the way the lights were numbered) was gone. But everything stage right of center was there. So we had to go through and put all the cues back into those lights that afternoon in two or three hours. And not only that, Frankfurt has a glass roof: It is, I think, one of the places that Speer built. There is daylight streaming in this arena all day, so not only do we have to do this quickly and under duress, we couldn't see worth shit. But we got it back together pretty well. Basically what it amounted to was that Tom Littrell and I knew what every light did all the time because we were constantly tweaking and repairing the show, and there were only forty Vari-Lites. But there was no way to save any of the show or go anywhere with any of it. It just lived in that console and it was refined day to day. So we go out to California to meet these cue memory cards and naturally there's nothing in them, it's bogus. So we had to reprogram the show out there too in the middle of the night for a couple of nights. As it turned out, it was hard, but it wasn't as tough as we feared. There was no way in the world that that was the way to run a railroad.

So that was the first time I remember somebody at Vari-Lite saying, "Well, we probably need a disk drive for this thing." I don't think we ever did get a reliable disk drive working for Series 100. They did have one for Series 200, as standard. So everybody could run floppies on their show. But—and I'm sorry to make this such a long way of answering— but that's the thing it turned out we needed the most that we didn't get for a long time.

Also, the time feature, which I mentioned earlier, the time control feature, to have time on all the functions, the fade and pan and tilt and so on—that didn't come for a long time either. The Series 200 came out with the next Genesis tour, which was the VL2 and the VL3, now defunct. In any case, they didn't have time on those for a long time. All of us who were enthusiastic users had been told that the time on the pan, tilt, and the time on the iris and the douser and all that would be on the Series 200. And it came out and it wasn't there . . . It wasn't there for a long time. I think it was another year or so. All of us—me more than a lot of people—had been doing more and more subtle, theatrical shows. I didn't do as much flash and bang as a lot of people did. In a Genesis show, they didn't miss the time feature that much because that was a lot more kinetic, even a violent kind of presentation. But I certainly missed it and some other people did, too.

LE TO TOM LITTRELL: *Would you say that your first console and then the 100 was the precursor to the Artisan, or was the Artisan a new and different thing?*

LITTRELL: They were very much the precursor. The Artisan just added more and more features. The whole notion of what theatre folks call loops and what we concert designers call chases were strictly an effect, a little bleeping marquee thing here and there. But with moving lights that becomes a far more sophisticated process. It already was far more sophisticated for concert touring because it was strictly part of the palette; part of the tools that you use when you're trying to paint that concert stage, to continue that artistic metaphor. We were already thinking in terms of a very sophisticated chasing, looping kind of feature to the console. The preconception about chases is that they're used for a trick, or a marquee chase, or twinkle lights—something you can do that's saved for the final big moment of the show. But the way chases are used with moving lights, it's a lot more subtle. It can be as much a part of the real quiet subtle things that you do, because when you've got a multifunction light, subtle changes in intensity and color happening at the same time and with slightly different timing values can make the stage undulate, or the lights can shimmer or the lights can shiver. You do that with really carefully built loops—it's not just a "one on/three off" marquee chase running at one hit a second. There are a lot of different timing values and a lot of different lights doing different things at different times in order to get that effect. With moving lights it can be very subtle and very wonderful, and it's a big part of the palette. The very first console didn't have that feature, but the Series 100 started us in the direction toward where the Artisan is now, which is a very sophisticated chasing setup.

BRANTON: They never had much success getting anybody in the theatre market interested in the lights until they got all those things [timing especially] solved. And solved the noise. They were incredibly noisy in the beginning. I mean all those things would move or change colors or something and it sounded like there was a car wreck outside. For the Series 200, they built noise baffles. Later, all the Series 300 gear was very, very quiet. And that's another thing you can't say for most of the competition. It's all just incredibly noisy. I was just on a show the other day that had a bunch of lights on it that I won't name, and God almighty, it was unbelievably noisy.

<u>LE:</u> *You mentioned yesterday that although changes have happened very quickly, overall progress hasn't been great. Can you elaborate on that a little bit? What kind of progress would you like to see?*

<u>BRANTON:</u> If you go back to your earlier question, of back in the beginning, what were the things that you guys said you would like to see, you people who were using this technology, that you would like to see that you didn't have, or what should the light do that it doesn't do? Well, basically it should do what traditional lights do, but automated—that's the long and the short of it. In other words, before this technology came along, even to do a simple rock show or a simple cabaret show like Diana Ross—never mind Broadway or television—I would have quite an elaborate body of tools to use: half a dozen different sorts of lekos, PARs, fresnels, barn doors, cyc strips, and so on. And then the purpose of each type was dependent on the task involved and knowing what you wanted to do. With a leko you want a light that's very controlled to do whatever the task is, and depending on how big the area is and the throw distance you picked a certain one, and you know there was just a hell of a lot of variation in it. And to build that much potential variation into one light is virtually impossible. The myth is that if you have some automated lights, you can cover all these bases and not have these traditional tools, and that's just not so. It's a lot closer to being true today than it was then, but boy, it's taken a hell of a long time to get there. We just got from Vari-Lite in January of '97 a lens kit for the VL6 that allows it to be what they call a medium throw. And before that, about a year earlier, we'd gotten a lens kit for it that allowed it to be a short throw or a wide angle. It reminded me of, in the old days, what I used to use a 4½ X 6 leko to do. So here we finally have a hard-edge light that will basically do, in terms of field control, anything that you would do with a traditional batch of ellipsoidals. Except it still won't shutter and it still

doesn't change colors except with a bang. It's still a very crude instrument. So, the techniques that you would see in any Broadway play—pick one—much of that couldn't be achieved very well with automated fixtures even now. [The VL1000 is said to address some of these concerns.] Because there's still not quite enough flexibility or precision in them nor is there enough variation between the different types to do all the tasks that you have to do.

> Manufacturers did make improvements that eventually made it feasible for moving lights to be used in more than just concert venues. These improvements included ease of control, noise reduction, color fading, some shuttering capabilities, more effects including gobo morphing, and others. Their function in the theatre tends to be somewhat different, however, than for concerts.

MARC B. WEISS: Moving lights are fabulous, but when I use them the lights usually move and change in the dark, so I have infinite specials with no refocus time. My design for *Music of Andrew Lloyd Webber in Concert* with Sarah Brightman and Michael Crawford opened in Vancouver with 250 conventional lights. It became hugely successful at the O'Keefe in Toronto, and a tour package went out with eighty conventional lights—mostly front of house—and twenty-one moving lights. If Vari-Lites had shutters, there could have just been fifty Vari-Lites and that would have been it. The Vari-Lites could be used for full color logos of the individual shows that then changed to backlight specials on the performers. Eventually it got down to a four-hour load-in so they were able to pick up an extra show each week—which paid for the cost of the moving lights. There were only a handful of places where the lights moved live. There was no "flash and trash."

LITTRELL: [Automation] is a tool. It's an incredible tool and it's like the computer on your desk. It does more than you ever imagined five years ago, but you already hate it because it doesn't quite do this or quite do that and because you've gotten more sophisticated about what you need. That is the challenge to us and every other automated lighting company: to continue to try to meet the needs of the users.

There's been change. In a sense, we put it out there and because nothing else existed, everybody learned how to use it. We were very fortunate in that respect because there were still a lot of weaknesses—but it was still the coolest thing around. Now the designers have a lot of options. They know what they want and it's our job to give it to them. And they're leading us where they need us to be. And by paying attention to that, Vari-Lites are no longer a kind of add-on special effect at a rock show; they are a primary lighting instrument for Broadway shows and West End shows and corporate events.

LE: *You mentioned on the phone the last time that* Will Rogers Follies *was the first, or one of the first, Broadway shows to use Vari-Lites?*

LITTRELL: Yes.

LE: *Interestingly enough, it was also one of the first shows to use DMX-controlled color scrollers. They had a lot of trouble with them. It was in the early days of DMX.*

LITTRELL: Well, like any other area there are those vanguard designers like Alan Owen and Allen Branton in the rock world, and you have got people like Jules [Fisher][5] and Peggy [Eisenhauer] in theatre that are looking for a new paradigm—let's get out of this paradigm and find something new. They think in that way: "What's new and how can we do things slightly differently?"

> After speaking with Littrell and Branton about the early days of the Vari-Lite, I began to explore the ways in which moving lights have in fact made their way into what is termed, rather prudishly, the "legitimate" theatre.

RICHARD WINKLER: I use moving lights as frequently as producers have the money to pay for them. I think they are wonderful things. I try to use them as part of the intrinsic design, as opposed to simply lights that can move around the stage—unless the show calls for lights that can just simply move around the stage.

LE: *When you say an intrinsic part of the design, what do you mean by that?*

WINKLER: I use them for specials, or to highlight things, or to enhance

---

5. Fisher won a Tony award for his design of *Will Rogers Follies*.

a performer's movement. But I don't like to just use them to make things flash and wiggle. Anybody can do that. That's not interesting to me. You don't need a designer to make that happen, to make things flash and wiggle.

LE: *The dealers do that in demonstrations.*

WINKLER: Exactly, to show what it is that their lights can and cannot do. And I love the lights and they give me great flexibility. They give you a great deal more power, obviously, because of the [high intensity discharge] source. So, they're good things.

NEIL PETER JAMPOLIS: I have to say that just because a light can move doesn't mean it should. I've gotten into using automation in quite an active way in the last few years, yet I could probably count on one hand the number of shows in which anyone ever saw the light move. Sometimes they do move live, and I soften them out and bury them, so that they are actually tracking somebody in a moment, and then resolving themselves when they get to the new position. . . . Because they can become *too* interesting. There was a whole period of lighting design—or of the theory of lighting design—that was that good lighting was lighting you didn't notice. And of course that probably evolved out of the fact that the lighting you did notice was terrible lighting. The last thing you want to think was, "What was this lighting going on?" So, I always thought everybody, including the lighting designer, owed the audience a show, but you don't want the show to be the lighting, I would hope. I suppose there's a certain kind of theatre where you do, but mercifully I don't have to do that.

DENNIS PARICHY: I've used moving lights only a very, very small amount. I'm not very familiar or at ease with them personally at this time [June, 1997]. In most of the places I work and for the shows I work on, they are either not really appropriate or the budget is never going to be there to use them, so I've only used them maybe seven or eight times. Actually, three months ago I did a show at Pittsburgh Public Playhouse—you might have heard of the show, *The Steward of Christendom*. It's a new Irish play, a memory play: an old man remembering his past around the time of the revolution in Dublin and the withdrawal of the British from Ireland. There are a lot of interesting memory scenes in the present and scenes going back and forth, and several characters are ghostly presences. They just happened to have two Cyberlights there. The artistic director[6] loves his Cyberlights—that's why they have them—he bought them because someone talked him into using them on *The Dybbuk* or something like that. He thought they were fabulous, so he had to invest money in them. They were there and I used them for these specials and these ghostly things. It was the first time I'd worked somewhere where they were just there as part of the inventory and it wasn't a struggle getting them, so I had a chance to use them with more care and with less concern. I used them in terms of "what can I do with them artistically in this circumstance?" I had plenty of time to do it and I didn't have to worry about not really being swift at programming them. There were only two of them, so it wasn't very complex. I began to see the possibilities of using them in dramatic plays. Every once in a while I've tried them and then I'd take them away because they somehow didn't quite blend in with the rest of the lighting. But for some moments they worked perfectly. So, I have mixed feelings about them. I used them once on one other play in similar fashion where I needed a lot of specials and it was just an easy way under the circumstance. But again, they didn't blend in very well. I wasn't able to get the color and color temperature and the quality of blending I wanted. The only other thing I've used them for in a small way is an awards show that I do every year where they're just merely flash.

LE: *Did you find on the two straight plays that they took an inordinate amount of time to program and cue them?*

PARICHY: That's the way I felt at the beginning. But actually one of the things that helped was that I had people who knew how to do it. So I would just say, "I want it over there" and I didn't have to really learn myself. Which is probably a bad thing, actually.

LE: *That's the way that it works in concert lighting, though—the designer says to the operator, "Move it over there," "Turn it red," and the operator figures it all out. In a way, that's how they have been designed to be used.*

---

6. Edward Gilbert was replaced by Ted Pappas after the 1999–2000 season.

PARICHY: That's probably so. I just feel like I ought to be able to control all that myself in the sense of telling someone exactly what I want, what operation I want him or her to perform. Rather than to say, "I need it to do this; can you make it do that?" to be able to say, "Channel 128, bring it up to 54," so that it is at my fingertips without any fumbling around.

LITTRELL: The whole relationship between the programmer and the designer changes when you deal with moving lights. The language changes too. It's no longer a command line type situation in a lot of instances. It's not "group 5, intensity 50, time 4, and store that as cue 11" and walk on to the next cue. It's in a lot of ways a philosophically different relationship: The designer and the programmer are more of artistic partners in the venture. The designer wants a blue-green watery shimmery thing, and he describes it as that to the automated lighting programmer to then break that down into numbers: "Let's see, I want my blue-greens going from 50 percent to 80 percent over about a three-second cross-fade, and I want to put a few pinks on top of that with a slightly different cross-fade." He starts and it's just a lot of little things that are going on in his mind number-wise to achieve this kind of blue-green watery shimmery thing that the lighting designer comes up with. It might be a cue for a forest scene from *Midsummer Night's Dream* or for the middle bridge of a four-minute rock song where it used to be big and loud and breaks down to soft and quiet. The techniques are similar. What differs though is the kind of intensity of the changes: For *Midsummer Night's Dream* it might be an intensity change of 40 percent to 50 percent and back and forth between those two, so that it looks this way; but for a rock song that breaks down to a quieter bridge, it might be an intensity change of 10 percent up to 85 percent, and instead of four seconds it's two seconds just to give it more dynamics.

LE TO MITCH DANA: *If you designed a production of* Joseph and the Amazing Technicolor Dreamcoat *in revival today, as compared with the production you did in the 1970s, how many dimmers and how much automation do you think it would have?*

MITCH DANA: I don't like to blow this stuff out too much, so it would probably be very close to what I have up now in *Faust* (at Opera Festival of New Jersey in a three-opera rep). Or, probably closer to what I have up in *Man of La Mancha* at the Paper Mill Playhouse. It would probably be around fifty scrollers, or it would have two dozen Studio Colors and about 250 focusing units. At the Paper Mill, I tend to put in 500 to 700 units, or records. I think *Secret Garden* had around 750 records. But then some of that is strip lights and some of that is scrollers, and all that other kind of stuff. We're running around 450 units, plus we had a dozen Vari-Lites, or half a dozen Vari-Lites and half a dozen Intellibeams, and fifty scrollers, and remote-control units on radio-control dimmers on platforms and turtles moving all over everywhere.

LE: *Did you control all of that from one console?*

DANA: Yes. At Paper Mill we've used a full Obsession—and I think the system works very nicely actually because we don't use hundreds of moving lights. And what we had been doing on *Secret Garden*, we were using a second Obsession front end as an auxiliary board. So it was the number two, here in multiuser it was number two. And seriously enough, we discovered a flaw in the board on that show that ETC had not discovered, even though this concept had been out for two years: The second board could not make parts. The primary board has to make the part. The secondary board can then write to the part. We were using parts in order to do setups on moving lights, and that's where we came up with the problem. Now what they use is an Impression 2X as the second board and it's slaved in on MIDI, and then they also have a digitizer pad. It's very fast and very clean, and it works extremely well for our kind of work. If we were using thirty lights or something like that, we would probably want to go to a moving light board.[7]

CURT OSTERMANN: I used Vari-Lites from the beginning on industrials, but only when it was for a specific kind of effect the producer was going after. From 1993 on, ever since the Cyberlight was introduced—actually, ever since moving lights came out that were DMX controlled, that you did not need to get special operators and special boards for (i.e., not Vari-Lites)—they have become de rigueur in the light plot. I would never con-

---

7. According to Dana, in 2000, Paper Mill Playhouse switched to using a Whole Hog for control of moving lights, a console designed specifically for that application.

ceive of doing an industrial now without some type of moving light. And I normally use Cyberlights just because Cyberlights and the Studio Colors don't need a special board; I can hook them into the same board I have for the fixed-focus lighting. I don't need special personnel to run those units. I can still use my electricians. It doesn't cost an extra airfare, doesn't cost an extra hotel room. And now that Vari-Lite has the VL5A and VL6, which can be controlled by a regular console, I am using Vari-Lites again, too.

I prefer the Expression 2X to control those and my second choice would be an Obsession.[8] That's just because I work now in "static" pictures. When I design a play, I usually think of the lighting as a beginning, middle, and end of one huge breath, so a tracking board makes perfect sense. But when I'm working for television or industrials, I'm looking at static pictures. Not that transitions aren't important, but once I get into a podium look or something like that, that is the "picture" for that segment, then I'm not interested in tracking boards. In fact, they get in my way. For example, I don't want elements of the podium look tracking though to the video look.

JEFF DAVIS: I just did a musical called *Play On*. I lit all of the scenery with automated lights. It was very odd because the scenery was a bunch of panels behind mirrored boxes, and it was very strange. So I basically used Studio Color units to light all the scenery. I only had five VL6's in it, doing the specials and template washes and stuff like that on the floor . . . and a bunch of color scrollers on pipe ends. That was the most amount of moving equipment I've ever used on a show. And a lot of it's because, to me, it has to fit the project. I feel part of my thing is that I love color mixing. I would much rather do that than scroll from one color to the next. I think mixing is richer; I think it's more interesting. And also I don't do a lot of big Broadway musicals; I don't work in places that have the budget to do it.

LE: *Ironically, there was a children's production of* Peter Pan *in Milwaukee this season[9] where Tinkerbell was played by a Cyberlight. That's something you wouldn't have seen three years ago.*

---

8. ETC's Obsession console is more like the Strand Light Palette series popular in the 1980s in that it operates on a "last-action" or "tracking" philosophy of control rather than on a "highest-takes-precedence" philosophy.
9. 1996–97.

DAVIS: Although when they did the Sandy Duncan revival on Broadway it was a laser.

LE: *Yes, but that was on Broadway, and this was at a children's theatre in Milwaukee; my point being that automation is pervasive—its spreading out all over the country.*

DAVIS: Well, that is interesting too, because it is like the computer board thing. Four years ago, or five years ago, the Intellibeam was the hot new thing. Now it's at the low end of the list: "I'll put up with that if I can't get a Cyberlight." The price has dropped so incredibly that a really small theatre can afford to rent them, which is a really a cool thing. Still, in my experience you can go into some places like the Old Globe in San Diego, and they don't have the money for that kind of stuff. They don't even have Source 4's yet. . . . I've learned, doing regional theatre, to do very nicely without all those flashy tricks. Although, you know, if I could drag an Obsession board with me every place I'd be happy.

LE: *Getting back to* Play On, *which was the example you gave me that you did with a lot of automated lights, did you do most of that changing in the dark?*

DAVIS: I actually did some live scrolls. And I laid it out that way to be able to do it. I laid those scrollers out very much like the spectrum so you could do a five-count fade from a light orange to a dark orange or the like. I had done the show in San Diego without any moving anything. So I basically put scrollers on the pipe ends and started out the show using the same colors that they were in San Diego. Then gradually I said, "Oh, that would be nice if this was red" . . . and added them into the show as we went. Some places I knew what I wanted to do, but sometimes I put them up and said, "this would be better if it were a richer color."

LE: *Did you use movement at all, with the VL6's and the Studio Colors, or did they only move when they were out?*

DAVIS: We did a couple of live movement things with the VL6's, but not very many, because I didn't ever want to make it into a lighting show. We didn't haze the air; we didn't do any of that stuff, except for one scene, the very opening of the show. Especially because of all the mirrored scenery and all the reflection, it was confusing enough to look at, without having to put beams of light into it. I used the Studio Color units to light the panels, and they all sat in different places within these mirrored boxes, depending on the graphic. So I was able to actually use the Studio Colors like PAR cans. The sets usually changed in the dark, so I was able to change the Studio Colors' positions in the dark. We did lots of color changes live, though. We did a lot of color fading, color bumping, and stuff in the scenery. So that's why I really chose those units as opposed to fixed units with scrollers, because I knew I had to be able to fade and bump colors for musical numbers.

BILLINGTON: Color changers have been around a long time, but what I think was the great invention was color faders—when Morpheus came up with color faders that could fade from color to color. Now that's pretty impressive . . . as one of the things you didn't used to be able to do.

One of the most extravagant uses of moving lights and scenic effects in the mid 1990s was on the Las Vegas extravaganza *EFX,* with lighting design by Natasha Katz and set design by David Mitchell.

LE TO NATASHA KATZ: *In a 1995 TCI article about* EFX, *your assistant is quoted as saying, "The show was lit primarily with moving lights, which was a surprise to everyone."[10] And I'm wondering what he meant by that.*

NATASHA KATZ: I don't know that it would be a surprise to me, but I think that meant that the show started to become specifically lit. . . . And the conventional equipment, if we want to call it that, which I guess everybody pretty much calls it, was very bread and butter: a lot of washes, backlight wash, sidelight wash. The stage is enormous—it's one hundred feet wide. So a sidelight wash is five or six lamps to get across the whole stage, and that very often just felt too broad, so by that being so broad, I'd have to turn it off, and then the moving lights would have to come into play because they are the ones that could really isolate things. There were not a lot of conventional specials and things like that

---

10. Ruling, Karl G. "EFX: A Unique Entertainment Redefines the Las Vegas Experience," *TCI,* August–September 1995, p. 34.

on the rig. So it is true—the moving lights do light the show, mostly. The conventional stuff is used to help with color temperature and costumes and big full-stage scenes and things like that.

LE: *You used the automated lights on top of the Pani-projected images?*

KATZ: Yes. We do a lot of that in the show, and I'm actually extremely proud of it to tell you the truth. . . . There's a false surround out in the audience, and there are four Pani projectors out front that light the surround. And along with the Pani projectors lighting it there are also the moving lights lighting it. For instance, the Pani might be doing planets moving or something like that which we do in the show, and then the Cyberlights are imposed on top of that in a star field. Then comes the subtler thing, which is that out of the side walls come the characters. In order to isolate them, I have to light them. But then you'd see a lot of . . . flares where the light dribbles off into nothingness. So, I would put a lot of texture around them with a moving light, which then blended in with the Pani projector, which is all different textures, and then that blended in with the Rosco screen that the set designer used. So there was a lot of texture on texture of three elements: whatever the scenic element was, the moving light element, and the Pani element. . . . I thought it was really well done. I'm very proud of that. And, we had scrollers on the Panis, so they were moving lights. So you might see the planets moving one way and the stars moving another way. We had all the ability to do all those things.

LE: *Part of the reason you had that ability was probably because of control, which is of interest to me, too.*

KATZ: The Artisan controlled the Vari-Lites. And the Obsession did control all the conventional lights. There were a lot of Cyberlights on the show, and that's what the Animator controlled. And, we had the David Hersey light curtains on the show, and we had a PowerBook control those. So actually we had three operators once the show started operating, and then we finally tied it all together to show control and it's just one button push. Actually, in many cases it's not even a button push, it's just a MIDI command.

One thing that I did find somewhat interesting on *EFX* is that everybody talks about how moving lights will add to your creativity; you can do whatever you want. But because the show is so big, in some ways the decisions about what the light had to look like had to be clearly defined from the beginning. If you spend four hours working on something that afterwards you look at and say, "Oh, God, that looks terrible!" it's not just a matter of turning off the cool backlight and turning on the warm backlight. You have to completely start over again—and that time isn't there. So in some ways automation narrows you down to actually having to decide earlier.

LE: *Do you think that's a good thing or a bad thing?*

KATZ: I think it is . . . a thing. . . . I wish that it didn't take so long to program that many lights, but it just simply does. In some ways that's good because you actually have to make decisions. You can't rely on the moving lights to answer your problems for you, which I think is what happens sometimes. You might think, "Oh, God, I don't really know how I'm going to light it. Try that light over there. Ah, I don't like that, try that one." That's actually not the way to approach moving lights, in truth. So, I think it's good on some level because you really have to know what you want it to look like beforehand.

WINKLER: [Automation] has opened up a great deal of flexibility, but it has also opened up a great deal of nondesign, at home, on the drawing board. Many people think they can solve it in the theatre. But if you don't solve it on the drawing board, you haven't solved it, as far as I'm concerned. If you're doing a new show and somebody changes something, I'm not saying that you're supposed to have figured out what they're going to change and have created the appropriate look for whatever it is that they're supposed to change. I'm talking about if you're doing a show and you know what is going to happen on the stage in advance, that's when the homework should be done. I see a lot of shows where designers use standard colors in their moving lights, and their color palettes in their conventional lights are totally different. And so in my head they haven't done all of their color work because things don't match and don't look like they belong together. The magenta that you can pick out of the Roscolux book, to have out of the dozen magentas that you can pick out of the Roscolux book—none of them match the magenta color in the Cyberlight. So all of a sudden you have a blue magenta, and then you could have a green magenta. And all of a sudden you look at the stage and you go, "Uhmmm, I don't quite get this." The majority of the world doesn't see this, doesn't perceive it, doesn't understand it, doesn't know why it is the way it is, and the majority of the world doesn't care. But if you're talking about pure design, I care.

Much as the designer working with piano boards had to be concerned about operability, a good designer today must be concerned with the programmability of their automated and fixed-focus lights. The "homework" the designer in the 1970s had to do to assure that cues could be executed manually on resistance dimmers has been replaced in the 1990s by homework characterized by a need to figure out where lights will move, what color they will change to, and when those changes can happen so as to be seamlessly integrated with the action of the play and the more "conventional" fixed-focus lights.

SECTION 3

The Evolution of a Standardized Protocol and the Accessibility of Automation

Interconnectivity between control consoles and lighting devices such as color scrollers and automated lights has had a dramatic effect on the lighting art and the lighting industry. Although the idea of "plug and play" is not a new one in the computer industry, it was not possible to implement that idea in the lighting industry until manufacturers agreed to standardize the way their control consoles sent data to dimmers and other devices. Once this was done in 1986 with the adoption of USITT's DMX512 Digital Data Transmission Standard, a greater range of automation devices were manufactured and integrated into theatrical usage. A transmission standard for control consoles ultimately meant that automated lights, which before the late 1980s could only be run on proprietary hardware, could now be operated from most any available console, making automation more accessible to theatrical users. Standardization also meant that the market opened up for new or growing manufacturers of computer consoles, dimmers, and peripheral devices.

<u>STEVE TERRY:</u> Interconnectivity is very interesting to look at philosophically. It certainly had an order of magnitude growth effect on the lighting industry. Just like when the computer showed up, you could have a show with nine thousand lights on it and have just one operator, with DMX you could connect nine thousand peripherals and color changers and moving lights. All of a sudden things that were accessories and specialty items became part of the generic toolbox. The parallel here is that

open system of interconnectivity model that you look at with the IBM PC; it's a very parallel evolution where if you make a standard that is wide open then everybody jumps on board, the thing builds momentum like a snowball, and it just gets larger and larger and larger.

That's the up side of it. The down side of it is that now DMX is called upon to do stuff that it never was designed to do. And the industry is now grappling with how to deal with that. But yes, that's a very interesting thought of yours that interconnectivity has caused a dramatic change in the industry. Which it really has.

It was the adoption by moving light manufacturers of a standardized control protocol, DMX512, that enabled theatrical designers to better integrate moving lights with conventional fixtures. Vari-Lites continued for some time to be used only with their own proprietary Artisan console's protocol, but many other manufacturers adopted DMX512 to enable theatrical lighting control consoles to drive their devices: both peripherals, such as color changers, and automated lights.

TERRY: It happened really in two parallel paths. Over here, the first accessories to get on the standard were color scrollers. The first color scroller of any kind of quantity in this market was the Color Wiz from Great American Market. And it was the first one that you could connect directly to your console. But it was an analog device. So, what would happen is that you had differences in calibration caused by voltage drop in the analog cable. If you had forty scrollers on the show, you had forty separate channels to get the thing to the right level. Then Keny Whitwright split off from Joe Tawil [of Great American Market, now Gam Products] and started marketing The Scroller under the Wybron name, which was the next generation product after Color Wiz. The first one came out in an analog version. And I said to Keny, "Keny, this is really atrocious. You're never going to make this work unless you get rid of all the variables in the analog control wiring. We've got to have one that accepts DMX512 directly." It was clear to me that if we could get that data into the scroller, and it was, for example, hexadecimal 55 coming down the pipe, it was going to go to the right color. So in the middle of the development of the scroller he added this little plug-in module so you could order the thing either way: analog or DMX. And our first experience with the DMX unit was on the road, the tour of *Chess*, for Tom Mallow. It was Ken Billington designing it and David Mitchell did the scenery. There were about seventy of these new scrollers on this show and, by God, you could put them all on the same channel, and say "Channel 1 at 50," and they all went to the same color. So that was a pretty amazing advance. Now we began to see what was possible here.

Then on the other end, in 1989, we were developing the projection system for Siegfried and Roy at the Mirage Hotel in Las Vegas, and we developed a brand new product called the A32 slide changer. It was a device which would change thirty-two slides through the gate of a Pani projector, and I said, "Well, let's use DMX." This was an implementation using five channels of DMX. Now, unbeknownst to us, in Europe, the moving mirror manufacturers had also adapted to the standard. They had seen it in *Lighting and Sound International*[1] and they said, "Wow, we can use this." Pulsar was designing all the electronics for Clay Paky, and they still do. Paul Mardon said "Well, OK, we have our Pulsar protocol PMX, but we could certainly make DMX work," so they put DMX on their moving lights. Then High End Systems started doing the same thing. After Intellibeams had been introduced, they made a version of the system that would—sort of—listen to DMX.

USITT's "DMX512 Digital Data Transmission Standard for Dimmers and Controllers" was developed in the mid 1980s as a dimming protocol, with relatively little thought given to automated lighting or control of peripherals. At its annual conference in Oakland in 1986, the Engineering Commission of USITT brought a group of people together to discuss the necessity and viability of creating a standardized digital control protocol. Prior to this meeting, the three largest dimming and control manufacturers, Colortran, Kliegl, and Strand, used proprietary protocols known as CMX, K96, and CD80 protocol, respectively. Smaller manufacturers, usually making either dimmers or controls, made black box interfaces to enable their products to "talk" to those of other man-

---

1. *Lighting and Sound International* is a publication of the Professional Light and Sound Association, a European trade organization analogous to ESTA, the Entertainment Services and Trade Association, in the U.S.

ufacturers. An analog multiplex standard, AMX192, was also discussed at this meeting. AMX192 standardized and made public Strand's CD80 protocol, enabling various manufacturers' consoles to talk to the then most popular dimmers on the market.

TERRY: If you look back to, say, 19 . . . 78 to '84, that was the time when the world was making a transition from analog dimming to digital control. And by the way, it's important to differentiate between digital dimming and digital control, you know. Digital dimmers came later with the Kliegl K96 and the LMI RD-2000, but each manufacturer was moving on to their various proprietary multiplexing schemes, and of course it created chaos. Manufacturers really liked that because it forced customers to buy things from one manufacturer. They had to buy dimming and control from the same manufacturer—Kliegl maintained a lock on their market, Strand maintained a lock on their market, Colortran on their market. And I remember catching an awful lot of flak. Manufacturers paid lip service to the fact that standardization was going to be a good thing, but that was not how they felt. They were basically forced into doing this by the rental market, the New York rental market. I received flak from everybody. Nobody wanted the standard when we first did it. First of all, nobody had ever had a standard before so nobody knew what to do with it. It was widely viewed with distrust: "What are these guys in New York trying to do?" Certainly Kliegl, Strand, and Colortran wanted no part of it. But, there was no choice. Basically, the three big New York rental shops got together and said, "Hey guys. . . ."

LE: *This was Production Arts, Four Star, and Vanco? Or . . .*

TERRY: Yes, P.A., Vanco, and Bash. I'm trying to think who else was really instrumental in that, in sort of forcing the issue here. A big part of it was Fred Foster at ETC and Al Pfeiffer at LMI, because those guys were in the soup. They had Fred building consoles and Al building dimmers, and every time we turned around LMI was having to produce another garbage little box, so we could plug a [Strand] Mini Light Palette into LMI dimmers, or a Kliegl Performer into LMI dimmers. And then they had yet another protocol which they agreed upon between LMI and ETC and it was chaos, it was total chaos. So those guys were interested in helping DMX move forward. It helped that we got an agreement from LMI and ETC that if we came up with a standard, they would immediately adopt it.

MITCH HEFTER: I can't remember exactly how the session came to be . . . it almost didn't, but I was pushed to keep it going. Roger Volk, who was the president of Teatronics at that time, was eventually listed as the session chair, and he did a lot of the coordinating, but I have no idea where he is these days.

LE: *You were with Strand then?*

HEFTER: I was with Strand. I suspect that was about the time when I became the manager of applications engineering. I was engineering commissioner of USITT at the time—that had happened the previous summer.

BILL FLORAC: We had a meeting at which we tried to take a method-ological step. We did DMX initially and we tried to make it an intelligent protocol. There was a meeting initially at USITT, and another meeting at Dallas or Chicago or somewhere more convenient . . . we got more done at the second meeting. . . . If it was at USITT, Roger [Volk] probably would have been there at the time.

LE: *Yourself, Steve Terry, Fred Foster, Gordon Pearlman . . . (just to refresh your memory), Ken Vannice from Colortran, and Brad Rodriguez from Strand. Tim Burnham [Arri] may or may not have been there. In the doc-umentation of the updates leading to the 1990 revision however, Roger Volk's name doesn't appear again.*

HEFTER: Teatronics started to drop out of things. Part of that happened because when they were going they made their own dimmers, but they bought their consoles from ETC, just as LMI did. And of course when LMI and ETC merged, which was a couple of years later, that merger even-tually cut off Teatronics' source of consoles. They worked on developing their own, but that may have been a factor in them starting to disappear. There was a company, ISH, that tried to revive Teatronics a few years ago.

FLORAC: I think Martin Moore was in it a little bit . . . and Mike Callahan, from Consolidated Edification and Sean Atkins from Pthalo Systems. Kirk may have been there, Kirk Hanson from Avo. I think

Mitch Hefter was there because he was very involved in the engineering aspect of USITT at the time. I don't think Dave Bertenshaw was involved. That's the person who would be from Strand Europe, but I don't think Europe had a lot of involvement at the time. Charlie Richmond came along a little later, I think . . .

It was a good time. I remember the meeting; I remember walking out thinking we had something in hand that was usable. I was in the audience as a manufacturer, as well as a lot of other people. It was a very small committee. It wasn't really a committee, it was a meeting, more than anything else, as I recall. I remember standing up and insisting we do higher baud rate.

LE: *Just to refresh your memory, there was an article in Theatre Crafts about the meeting that said, "Software engineers who build black box go-betweens"—which is yourself—"were rendered false at a panel meeting chaired by Roger Volk, president of Teatronics. The announced purpose of the meeting was to decide whether or not to form a committee. But since those attending the meeting were the same people who would have formed the committee, several steps were skipped. The assembled multitude decided then and there to adopt a transmission standard that is pretty close to most systems now in use, but different enough to preclude giving any one company a competitive advantage. Most of the credit for this push probably has to go to representatives of the New York lighting rental houses"—you know who that is—"who stood up, waved a sheaf of papers, and said no one was going to issue any more purchase orders until there was some sort of standard, an effective technique apparently."*[2]

FLORAC: That's not how it happened [laughter]. I think there were some connotations of it, prior to that meeting. Steve was fishing with everybody, trying to get everybody to do something. There was a small panel . . . USITT was the only convention there was at the time. There were about twenty or twenty-five people representing manufacturers and people listening. . . . It wasn't a committee meeting at that time; it was just an open panel to discuss it. . . . I was sitting in the first row of chairs in the audience, there were a few people sitting up front, and then all the manufacturers' representatives were in the first row of the audience.

2. Sisk, Douglass. "USITT Product Roundup," *Theatre Crafts*, August/September 1986.

HEFTER: There were a lot of sales-type people around the room, standing at the back walls. It was a pretty big session. And I just remember watching some of them be pretty nervous about this, because everybody was all set on the proprietary protocols and there seemed to be concern that this would be bad for business, when in fact it turned out to be good for business. Nobody expected DMX to do what it did.

LE: *What was their argument against standardization?*

FRED FOSTER: The whole commercial argument against standardization and for proprietary protocols is this: If I'm company X, I'm the only one who can make things that plug into my system. You want a whole lighting system. In the case of Strand, or in the case of ETC now—if we caught that attitude—if you want our sets of dimmers and our Obsession console, you have to buy the whole package from us. No Obsession console without the dimmers. And the reality is that most companies, at least on the conventional side, make their money on the dimmers, not on the consoles or the spotlights necessarily. So you want to get the whole system. That's the commercial argument for proprietary protocols. Then you have to say to yourself, Do you really make more money by letting the customer pick and choose and be able to plug and play what they want? When ETC was just a console manufacturer, it made absolute sense, 100 percent commercial sense, to have a standard protocol, because then we could plug into anybody's dimmer and people could choose our console over Strand or Colortran or Kliegl. It was the same situation with Lighting Methods when they were just a dimming company. Who cares, you know, we can plug and play. And at that point in time it was such a nightmare . . . not only that, but we had the problem of trying to listen to everybody and talk to everybody. So it was just such a quagmire and confusion, for the business. For the business, standardization helped it tremendously.

TERRY: We were at that meeting at USITT where all the rental houses stood up and said, "You guys get your act together or we're not buying any more equipment." And basically Gordon Pearlman drafted the wording in principle of what it would be, which was a serial protocol with 8-bit level data utilizing a break as the marker between frames; basically an approximate verbal description of the Colortran protocol. So everybody turned to Ken Vannice of Colortran and said, "OK, Ken, how do you feel about that?" They had been really proprietary about that protocol. When they were doing their various memory systems and their various dimming systems, that was a big secret. You weren't allowed to talk about what that protocol was. Of course, it was dead simple. An agreement in principle occurred there, because Gordon was still on the Kliegl bandwagon at that point.

BRAD RODRIGUEZ: You get different attitudes from engineers than from marketers. Most engineers of my knowledge, unless they're nursing a pet idea of their own, would rather start with something that's known to work. You take something that is known to work, make some changes to it, standardize on that. It is a tremendous job to try to invent a standard out of whole cloth, so to speak, completely starting from scratch, without having any experience with it out in the field. It's very uncomfortable to go into something like that and try to get people to standardize on it before it's been field proven.

In email correspondence with me, Ken Vannice traced the development of the protocol on which DMX512 was eventually based to Colortran's "Dimension Five" console of the early '80s and the Channel Track of the late '70s. The Dimension Five had 256-step resolution and supported 512 channels with an update rate approximating 27 times per second.[3] The Channel Track console used a digital serial multiplexed interface for communication between the console and a digital-to-analog converter at the dimmers. This system had been designed by Fred Foster, who recounted its development in relation to the beginnings of ETC.

FOSTER: To follow the control thread—one of the things that my brother looked at changing was the architecture of our first system, the Mega Cue. Everything we had here was wire per dimmer. It was worse because of [being based on] the Q-File; it was one control wire going down to the dimmer, and then the feedback wire. There was a small step-down transformer and a mimic panel, which was just an incandescent light dimmed by the dimmer, and so there was this big bundle of wire. One

3. Ken Vannice, email to author, August 19, 1998.

of his early concepts was to replace the wire-per-dimmer link with a serial data cable—and Mega Cue actually had this. It had a dimmer interface in it, which was a box that wired into the existing dimmer in the dimmer per circuit. But then it had a coax cable between that and the console, which carried 156 kilobaud, actually 7-bit data between the console and the dimmers. Which in concept was really very close to the precursor of DMX, because rather than a break—which is just an extraordinarily long pulse without any transitions—for a marker it used a full, a 256, or an FF as a reset, and then valid levels were between 0 and FF, or 0 and 128. So you had 128 steps. But essentially it was a reset pulse, then 512 dimmers, then a reset pulse, then 512 dimmers again. So that was in existence in 1975 in the Channel Track, or in fact in Mega Cue, in '76 when we used it. And then when we did Channel Track it still had that architecture, but Colortran didn't want to market that. They were afraid people would say, "You mean there's one wire in here . . . and if that gets cut my system doesn't work?" So Channel Track had this big box console that was this wide [spreads his arms] that you could remove from the chassis, that had a manual scene above it, and connecting this big box that had the disk drive and processor, and the link between that and the dimmer interface unit, which was built into another part of the console, was still this serial data cable. But they hid it in this big box and they very rarely sold it as a remote device. Then they hired an internal group to start developing a memory system of their own. They were getting fed up with us. I'm trying to remember the name of the guy . . . Mark . . . he worked with Dimension 5, which was a product that Colortran developed for a while; it had eight fader wheels on it. Working with Colortran, he actually came up with a protocol that they started calling their DMX protocol, or rather Colortran—CMX— which was 156 kilobaud, which was the same bit rate or baud rate as the Channel Track protocol, but changed in that it wanted to get 8-bit resolution in the levels. He was the one who came up with the concept of putting in a break character as the reset character. So he really defined the header, the break, the null, and such.

We continued with the serial stuff; we took it as far as the Channel Track protocol. Then Colortran did their version of it, the CMX version. We did the ELC consoles for Disney, which was actually distributed processing where the console calculated all the channel information and sent channel levels down to the dimmer interface unit, the dimmer interface unit had the patch downloaded to it, and it actually did the soft patch calculations. So that let us use more channels and a higher refresh rate on channels going down, and the dimmer interface unit was doing a level of conversion.

LE: *The dimmers were any manufacturer's dimmers?*

FOSTER: Any manufacturer's. We still didn't make dimmers, so the dimmer interface unit was a converter, a digital-to-analog converter; it spewed out 0 to 10 volts. We actually could at that point read back from a console and pump it back up over the digital line, so it was a bidirectional digital link. For Disney we developed all of that, but that was our own proprietary protocol. It was RS422,[4] which was a precursor to the RS485 data levels that are used for DMX. At the same time Kliegl did the K96 system, which took the distributed processing even further in that the processors and the dimmer racks can actually calculate the fades. So with the Entertainer console they had this little analog doohicky; all the cues were stored down in the dimmer racks and calculated in the dimmer racks. The fades were actually calculated there, not just the soft patch as we had done, or what Strand was doing which was to have the dimmers be essentially passive devices, just responding to signals. So those were the three significant efforts towards serial communication being done at that point. When we teamed up with the LMI and Teatronics, we found that Teatronics was cloning the CD80 product, so they had T-mox, which was a version of AMX, or the CD80 protocol, which at least was double-ended, so it was a little bit noise-immune. And Lighting Methods was working on a digital control. They had actually made a card that fit inside a Performer, then took the analog signals from the Performer, put it into an LMI protocol, spewed it out of RS485 . . .

LE: *That was Micro II . . . ?*

FOSTER: Yes, the Micro II thing. In any case, it was an RS422 digital protocol that LMI developed. And their dimmers had the ability to store

---

4. RS422 and RS485 are standard serial data transmission protocols.

some backup looks as well. So they had intelligence in their dimmers at that point. So what we did when we started working with LMI is that we tweaked our digital protocol and their digital protocol and came up with the ability to have our consoles download our soft patch into their electronics, and so their electronics replaced our dimmer interface unit. And so that developed the ETC/LMI protocol, which was a combination of the one we did for Disney and LMI's. We kind of transmogrified them and jammed them together. For Teatronics we created a card that fit in our dimmer interface unit that spewed out T-mox, which was their analog protocol.

LE: *And this is around 198 . . . 5 . . . ?*

FOSTER: 1982, '83, '84, in that range. At the same time, the last console we did for Colortran was Patchman, in which we implemented the Colortran protocol. So we knew how to do the Colortran protocol. I think it got done before their console did, so it was the only thing they had that could speak this protocol. So, then it was at the 1986 USITT where there was the panel that was discussing serial protocols. . . . It must be interesting hearing each version of the story of that meeting.

LE: *Tell me yours.*

FOSTER: As I recall, everybody was talking around, and Ken Vannice couldn't make a corporate statement. Whoever was there from Strand was in the same boat. Nor did they really want to. And we kind of talked around it, and then I remember Gordon [Pearlman] huffing about something, saying "Come on. We know what the D192[5] protocol is." So he did one verse of it, then Flash [Bill Florac] threw in a piece, then I threw in a piece or somebody else. So by this time we had completely described this trade secret of Colortran's. And everyone turned to Ken and said, "Isn't that right, Ken?" And he just shrugged down. We came to the consensus that that was a pretty elegant protocol, it was easy to implement, and that perhaps we should go along that line.

LE: *I get the impression that the agenda for the 1986 meeting was not to write and adopt the protocol but instead to develop a timetable.*

---

5. D192 was Colortran's name for its serial multiplex protocol, which was later referred to as CMX. It is the protocol on which DMX512 is based.

HEFTER: Yes, that sounds correct. The agenda was basically: "Let's figure out how we can address this issue so the users don't have to fight multiple protocols when they try to run their spaces." One thing led to another and then we had a standard.

LE: *What was the mood at that original meeting?*

FLORAC: I don't recall the atmosphere. I think the atmosphere was generally gentle. I don't recall anybody yelling or screaming. I remember that when I stood up and said we had to do a faster baud rate, that everybody else said, "Oh, no no no." Especially Colortran, because they didn't want to change anything. We had done a protocol using an Avo console and it had a very fast chase in it, and I wanted to meet that chase. . . . We had done an interface between an Avo console and our LMI dimmers. The sample [DMX] rate was such that it wasn't fast enough. If someone wrote a chase, it would miss some of the lights; we had experienced this problem. So we figured that a 4-megabaud rate, which was the top rate at the time, would be barely fast enough to meet the Avo console. At the time it was as fast as you could go. The chip, the UART[6] we were all using, would go as fast as 4 megahertz, so that's the clock rate that was chosen.

HEFTER: One of the things that was going to be painful to everybody [in 1986] was that this was based on Colortran's protocol. However, the fact that we changed the clock speed meant that they couldn't just throw a switch, they had to go back and do some work. They might have had a little less to do than other manufacturers, but in fact they weren't even the first ones out with a DMX product; my recollection is that EDI actually shipped the first one.

At the time of the adoption of DMX512, Dave Cunningham's company Entertec was designing products for Colortran.

DAVE CUNNINGHAM: It screwed us up more because we already had the design. It was basically the Colortran standard protocol but [the standard] modified the baud rate to disfavor Colortran and not give

---

6. Universal Asynchronous Receiver/Transmitter.

Colortran an advantage, because it was already built into a number of the products. For a while after that there was a coexistence of the two protocols, and they were identical except for the baud rate.

LE: *Did you develop the protocol on which DMX was based?*

CUNNINGHAM: No. What happened was that there was some other product that had a serial output, and what I did was I took that and said, "You've already got that product in your product line, so why don't we use the same data protocol and data stream. . . . Let's use 422 at this data rate. Then it would be at least compatible with one other product in the product line." So that was the reason for choosing that. The DMX protocol is a standard serial protocol (422, I think) and then all you have to do is choose the baud rate and the data stream, the start byte and the 512 channels following.

Brad Rodriguez represented Strand at the Oakland meeting. He was responsible for writing the analog control standard, AMX192, based on the Strand CD80 protocol, also adopted at the 1986 meeting.

RODRIGUEZ: There wasn't that much discussion on the analog protocol. It was just, "Great . . . we're off." It wasn't a new protocol; it was an existing protocol that was in wide use. Basically all that had to be done was Strand had to say, "This is the official specification for the protocol," and everybody else said, "Great, we adopt it." The analog protocol was seen as the previous technology. It wasn't the area of hot competition. The digital protocol was what we saw as the future. This was where the competition was going to be. So we really wanted to—I think I am speaking on behalf of the non-Colortran manufacturers—we really wanted to make sure we were all starting off even.

I don't know that there was much discussion of AMX at that meeting. It was just, "Thank goodness Strand has finally put it on paper, and yes, we all accept it." There wasn't any argument because everybody acknowledged that Strand had invented it and everybody basically wanted to claim compatibility with Strand at that point. And so AMX192 was accepted without argument. DMX512 was a different story. Strand at this time had decided that we needed a digital protocol. That was the wave of the future. Even then, analog protocols had problems: You had ground loops; you got noise on the line. Diagnosing those in the field was a pain. K96 had come out. Colortran had their D192 (later it was called CMX). Strand needed a digital protocol. A couple of other companies were either trying to support Colortran or wanting to develop their own. So there was a lot of interest in a digital protocol. The purpose of that meeting was to define one that all the manufacturers would agree on. K96 was not suitable for technical reasons because K96 expected too much in the dimmers, if I recall correctly—and believe me I am no authority on K96. But as I recall, with K96, the actual soft patch was done in the dimmers. And so K96 was sending channel information and not dimmer information and thus required intelligent dimmers that could do a soft patch, and that's not what people wanted. They wanted basically a digital something like AMX192, just sending out dimmer information. There was some talk about what it would have to do and what data rate it would have to support and how many dimmers would lock on the link. Somewhere along the line, somebody—I don't remember who—basically said, "Well, there are two existing digital protocols, K96 and Colortran." And K96 for technical reasons wouldn't work; it wasn't what we wanted. And somebody at some point in the meeting said, "Why don't we just adopt the Colortran as the standard?" And . . . how to put this? [laughter] There was some resistance to this because some of the other manufacturers thought this would be giving Colortran too much of an edge. That they already had equipment out there supporting it, the rest of us were going to take a year to produce it, and so they'd have a one-year lead time on getting the market. And so, while we liked it in principle, we had to do something to level the playing field, as the modern expression goes. So, somebody else . . . from LMI . . .

LE: *Bill Florac.*

RODRIGUEZ: Thank you. Yes. He wanted to increase the baud rate. He said the problem with the Colortran protocol is it can only send, I think, twenty refreshes a second, and while that was fine for theatre, for live entertainment, for rock and roll or anything like that, it wasn't enough. That was the great compromise. Somebody said that they would increase it to 250 kilobauds. I think it had been 162.5 kilobauds or something like that. They would increase it to 250. And that made Bill happy, and the other people who wanted to have a faster refresh rate. That made the other manufacturers happy because we knew that the Colortran hardware wouldn't handle that, so we're all back to the drawing board. I, as a representative from Strand, said, "I'm happy." We did not want to go to the work of developing a protocol of our own if there was an acceptable one available to use. I went into the meeting with the philosophy that we will adopt whatever this meeting comes up with, unless they come up with something that's totally un-implementable. So I basically said on behalf of Strand that we would adopt it.

The point of that meeting was to come up with a protocol. That was why we were there. We wanted to come up with a protocol that we could all use. Whether or not an actual document was drafted and written there, we at least would agree on what the protocol would be. And at one point I made the comment that Strand was about the only company there without a vested interest, because we had nothing in digital already. Colortran had theirs, Kliegl had theirs, and a couple of other companies, like LMI, supported the Colortran already, so they had a head start on using that protocol. We were the only ones there I think that didn't have any digital protocol of any form whatsoever. And I said as much. I said we're willing to work with whatever you come up with. I should have done my homework a little better. There turned out to be some headaches with DMX512, but those have gone away. At the time it was hard to find a chip that would generate serial data that fast.

LE: *And how did you resolve that?*

RODRIGUEZ: There were a few. I think everybody in the market wound up using one of the very few chips that would generate serial data at 250 kilobauds, and of course with the march of microprocessor technology now there's a great number of chips that'll do that. We wound up using a chip from Signetics. I don't think it was a Motorola chip. General Instruments—or something like that—made the fastest chip on the market. There were only a few chips that would generate that data rate and had we known that at the time, we might have said, "Let's use a smaller number, make it DMX 256—fewer dimmers out and use a lower data rate and refresh." That's a side issue—I didn't know that at the time—so I said 250 kilobaud sounds fine to me. That was the compromise, and I left that meeting basically saying, "Whatever we come up with, I'm going to take that and start implementing it."

FOSTER: I think it was Flash who suggested that the Colortran protocol was inadequate because there were consoles on the market, notably the Avolites rock-and-roll desk, that had a 40-hertz update rate on the chasers. And you couldn't do 512 dimmers at 150 kilobaud at 40 hertz, so that was how he came out with the number of 250 kilobaud, or whatever the number is, that would accommodate that refresh rate. . . .

FLORAC: I think Strand had the biggest change probably of anybody else. They were technically ahead of us and had to jump back further than anybody else, in some aspects. . . . I only say that because—although I didn't know it at the time—when they came out with SMX a few years ago, they had been working on this for a long time but they weren't on the market.

LE: *Was there concern at Strand that Colortran's protocol had been adopted as DMX512?*

HEFTER: Not that I heard. That doesn't mean there may not have been concern, but I never heard that. And again, one of the things that was emphasized was that everybody had to go through some pain.

RODRIGUEZ: Let me try to give you the picture: I was the R&D software manager for Strand U.S. Strand U.S. and Strand U.K. were two independent organizations, which they attempted to merge in the mid '80s, and that was about the time I left the company, and all sorts of weird things happened then. But before that happened we had separate R&D operations, and in the U.S. there were three divisions. There was a vice president of R&D and then three managers below that: mechanical, engineering, and software. The software manager was in charge of the programmers. This put me in charge of console development. The engineering guy was doing dimmers and the mechanical guy was doing fixtures.

LE: *And who was the VP of R&D?*

RODRIGUEZ: When I joined the company it was Dave Cunningham, and then it became John Pavicek, if I recall correctly. Dave left and went on to work with Colortran and formed Entertec, and he went on to develop dimmers and consoles. At some point along the line, Leif Larsen (when I joined the company he was the engineering manager) got bumped up to be head of all of R&D.

FOSTER: In the late '70s, Strand developed the analog DMX, which was actually—as I understand it by talking to Dave Cunningham, whose group was responsible for defining it—the protocol they used to scan all the switches in the face panel. It had nothing to do with dimmer output, but just scanned all the switches. Rather than have to run all these wires down to individual input, they would have them all wired together on one common, and then—and I don't remember exactly how to do it—read each switch one at a time. They had pressure because Kliegl had introduced K96, its digital protocol, and they said, "Oh my God, we need a fewer-wire protocol." So they came up with this analog multiplex, which was just that console thing turned-sideways-and-spit-out-the-back control protocol. It was really horribly unreliable. It was a single-ended analog signal, so it was really subject to noise, and every one of their products had a different dialect of it, which was very difficult from a reverse engineering standpoint; even the compatibility of one of their products to another product wasn't very reliable.

> The variety of dialects was resolved somewhat at the 1986 Oakland conference when Strand put their CD80 protocol into the public domain and it was adopted as the AMX192 standard for analog multiplexing.

FOSTER: We ran into the politics of Strand—obviously, they wanted to win too—so we decided that the politics were probably fair if we made the official AMX protocol Strand's and got Strand to admit what the timing windows were, and the DMX protocol [was based on Colortran's].

HEFTER: I don't recall [those politics]. It may not be inaccurate, but it was more that at that time, the CD80 protocol was everywhere. Strand at that point was just huge and several people had reverse engineered the CD80 protocol. Part of the problem with CD80 is that there were variants on that protocol itself. If you took a console that was made in 1980 and took a dimmer cabinet that was made in '87, there might actually have been some communication problems because some of the timing windows shifted. Brad Rodriguez and I worked on that, although it was mostly Brad. The AMX192 standard is the best fit of those variations. So that's why if something speaks AMX192, there may be some versions of CD80 out there with which it still doesn't want to communicate. So, I'm not sure the statement that this was a counter to the Colortran standard is accurate. It was because of the variations of CD80; it was "let's get something nailed down that we can all stick to."

CUNNINGHAM: The original AMX protocol was something I did for Multi-Q. I just came up with it myself. They must have documented it later.

LE: *According to the people I talked with, nobody documented it until 1986 when AMX192 was written.*

CUNNINGHAM: It was on the original Light Palette [in 1979], although it had both outputs. It was one of those things where we didn't know if people would buy multiplexing, so it had both the analog outputs and multiplex outputs.

RODRIGUEZ: AMX192 was originally the CD80 protocol. The CD80 was a very successful product for Strand. Lots and lots of CD80 dimmers were being sold, so lots of other companies were making CD80-compatible products. The dimmers would take the CD80 signal from a Light Palette, from Mantrix, or consoles that would drive CD80 dimmers. There was a bit of confusion, because Strand had never published the CD80 specification for the control protocol. So people were trying to reverse engineer it by looking at what the consoles were producing, but there was some variation from the consoles, so sometimes it didn't work. Sometimes the timing was not quite right. Somebody at USITT thought it would be a great idea if we could just set down once and for all what the timing values were. I thought that was a great idea. Basically they wanted to standardize on what Strand was doing, and my job on the Strand side was to figure out exactly what Strand was doing. It turned out that it had never been formally specified within Strand.

There were two different documents describing the timing and the signal levels. There were some slight differences between the documents—and this is even within Strand.

LE: *So consoles such as the Mantrix and the Light Palette didn't actually speak the same thing. Is that true?*

RODRIGUEZ: They were producing a slightly different signal. There was actually a document for what the CD80 dimmer was expecting, a document for what the Mantrix was producing. I did the software for the Mantrix 2 so I was familiar with that second one. I took those two and wrote a document that basically reconciled them. And that was the draft of AMX192. You will notice in the AMX192 it actually has a specification for what the console must produce and a little bit more lax specification for what the dimmer must receive. That was to accommodate all the existing Strand consoles that I could find information on. Because, like you said, the Light Palette and the Mantrix could be producing slightly different timings.

LE: *Was the AMX192 protocol written in response to Kliegl's K96 protocol?*

RODRIGUEZ: No, there was no competition. AMX192 was an analog effect, it was last year's technology. When K96 came out, yes, Strand was worried about it. Worried may be overly strong, but Strand basically said, "We need a digital protocol." Strand had no digital protocol at that time and they realized that AMX192 was not going to compete with a digital protocol. In my judgment, if DMX512 had not come along right then, Strand would have gone on to develop a digital protocol of their own. AMX192 was in response to all the manufacturers that were making what they called CD80-compatible equipment that sometimes got out into the field and didn't work. And that was a headache for our guys: If you buy manufacturer A's console and manufacturer B's dimmer, and you put them together in the field and the system doesn't work, each manufacturer points a finger at the other one. We had something of an advantage because we could say, "You know, this is the CD80 and if the other manufacturer's stuff claims to be CD80-compatible, then that's their problem, not ours." But there was still a desire to get rid of all those little problems.

LE: *And, I imagine, to get rid of all the black box interfaces.*

RODRIGUEZ: Yes. From my point of view it was a feather in the cap for Strand to say that the whole industry's going to standardize on the protocol we invented. All the other manufacturers had the incentive that they wanted this timing specified once and for all so they wouldn't have to reverse engineer it and so they could say they were compatible and have some assurance that it would work. At least one marketing person in Strand was horrified at the idea that Strand was basically going to put its protocol out into the public domain. He seemed to think that this was a big marketing edge: If you wanted to buy CD80 dimmers, which everybody wanted at the time—it was a hot seller—you had to buy that console, or vice versa. Well, the vice versa wasn't so much, but if you wanted to drive CD80 dimmers, you needed one of our consoles. They thought this was a great marketing edge, a closed standard. You get this in the computer industry a lot also. With an open standard, there's more competition; with a closed standard you're trying to lock people into your product, and he thought we were going to lose that lock. But the engineering guys were saying that this will take a lot of problems away, take those problems off of our shoulders.

FOSTER: Up to this point, we were madly making our consoles talk to everybody else's product; Lighting Methods was making their dimmers listen to everybody else's. It was all done very haphazardly. We knew what Colortran's protocol was because it was evolutionary to begin with, and we had implemented it. We had to reverse engineer the others' protocols. Actually, LMI was the first group to reverse engineer the K96 protocol. And everybody had to reverse engineer the CD80 protocol, because the CD80 dimmer was by far the most prolific or ubiquitous product, so this was what everybody wanted to talk to. Strand's control consoles were the best or most commonly used, so everybody wanted to listen to them. So what was really interesting was at the time, as we would add friends to our team—Teatronics or Lighting Methods—we would get their empirical results out of reverse engineering as well as ours. Everybody started, as we had, to share this information. We started figuring out what the timing windows were, because Strand was holding this information incredibly close to their chest, obviously. So we started developing a pretty good idea of what the windows were, but not the official window. And it was just a nightmare. Every job that was a CD80 job, you would have to go out and tweak timing values, and it was just horrible.

<u>LE TO BRAD RODRIGUEZ:</u> *Prior to the 1986 conference, was there any agreement amongst anyone that you know of regarding AMX192?*

<u>RODRIGUEZ:</u> I don't remember who originally approached me with the question of "would Strand put the CD80 protocol into the public domain?" It might have been Steve Terry, but I don't remember. I bumped that up to the management and they basically, for whatever reasons, said, "Yes, we have no problem with it." And all that AMX192 was supposed to be was a codification of existing practice: "This is what we're doing, this is what everybody else is doing, these are the official timing specs, tweak your equipment to fit this." As I said, the meeting was to discuss dimmer standards, and that one had already been written. The consensus, I suspect—and I don't know because I didn't meet with many people beforehand—was that everybody just wanted CD80 to be written down on paper. This is when the Strand marketing guy was horrified . . . I think it was Kam McCormick, but I'm not sure; he was standing in the back of the room and no one had told him that we would be doing this, and I basically stood up and said, "Well, Strand is willing to put the CD80 protocol into the public domain and . . . I've written it up." And then he had this look of complete shock, because no one had warned him that was coming. As I recall, the basic reaction was everybody was happy: "Great, CD80 . . . well, let's just use that." They were very happy that Strand was willing to release the spec on CD80, and that formalized it, and everybody said, "Great, we'll adopt that, no problem." So I don't think that was in reaction to Colortran being proposed as the standard, because at the time we'd made the decision, Colortran hadn't even been suggested as the standard. There may have been—and this would be entire speculation on my part, I never heard anything to indicate this—there may have been discussions at the management level of Strand saying essentially, "We're stuck with an analog spec; Colortran's got a digital multiplex; how can we regain a marketing edge?" And the only thing they could come up with was, "Well, we can

make our analog a standard and that would regain a marketing edge over the other guy having digital." But that's pure speculation on my part, and I never heard anything to suggest that. I think the real motivation for Strand was basically recognition that everyone was using it anyway and wanting to avoid the kind of field problems we were having with dissimilar equipment.

LE: *Had there been some discussion about the standardization of the digital protocol prior to the Oakland meeting?*

FOSTER: There had been a whole lot of discussion leading up to the meeting about what the political maneuvering should be, behind the scenes, and how this could be done, and how the little guys could go after big companies who were trying to protect their markets and that sort of thing.

LE: *And you were in the "little guy" category at that time?*

FOSTER: Oh, yeah! Absolutely. System integration made a lot more sense to me back then than it does now. Steve [Terry] was posturing too, starting to use a line he still uses, and has used recently with Ethernet, which is "If you don't do this I won't buy your stuff,"[7] and putting market pressure on us nasty selfish manufacturers to do it as well. So the upshot is that at the end of the meeting there was a pretty clear direction on what to do, where to go, and I don't even know all the details after that except that I know that Colortran had to officially bless the effort and Strand had to, so that took some time. But by that time everybody was already implementing these things. So that's kind of how it all happened. At least from my recollection.

FLORAC: There was a lot of talk about it in advance. Basically, I think that Steve Terry of Production Arts being one of the—at that time—biggest dealers got real tired of having to play the interface box game. I think all the dealers and the customers insisted that we all get together and figure it out . . . it started that way, anyway. Steve Terry was a big client of ours and a big client of Strand's and a big client of Colortran's. And we all wanted to please Steve. So Steve said we're going to do this,

---

7. At the time of Fred Foster's interview, Terry was still vice president for lighting systems with Fourth Phase.

and we did it. I remember sitting up in one meeting, I don't know which meeting, and trying to explain why we needed to do this. I had one of our little interface boxes ETC made or LMI made. I brought it into the meeting and I said, "The reason we have to do this is so I don't have to make this product anymore." I held it right up in my hand and everyone had a good laugh at it. You know, because basically . . . [we] didn't have a protocol at the time. We sat in the meeting trying to find a common ground. We had these great ambitions of creating a good protocol, and kept whittling it down and whittling it down to make it easy for a client to adapt to. It turned out to be a very basic protocol, which is good and bad. . . . We ended up pretty much picking up Colortran's protocol, but at my insistence bumping the baud rate a little bit—one, because we needed to do a better classification of timing windows; two, whether we had to change our protocol it made it harder or easier to adopt; and three, we had to have Colortran change something. It was one of those few times where things clicked along pretty well, all of the proceedings involved.

LE: *Was there resistance at that meeting? Later there was some resistance from consultants and suppliers after the meeting, but . . . at the time, I would imagine Colortran, Strand, Kliegl weren't as keen on this as LMI, ETC, Teatronics, dealers.*

FLORAC: They were not. . . . As you say, the dealers really wanted it. I don't think there was any question that that was driving it. Anyone who was coming at it from a marketing point of view had a real problem because, from their perspective, if we made it universal, you could sell your consoles with my dimmers, and they didn't want that. And hindsight has shown us that it's been the best thing for the market. No one got hurt by it really. But . . . in subsequent standards of trying to do better protocols, the same issues have arisen: "You don't want a standard in a moving light protocol, because of the console." We should learn our lessons in that the same issues are involved.

RODRIGUEZ: I think one of the advantages that DMX had is that we were basically saying: We're taking a field-proven spec and changing the data rate, and all the engineers knew that changing the data rate did not make a fundamental difference in how it would work. It would be faster, but it's the same protocol and it has worked and it's been used. That was a big argument for it, that it was based on an existing protocol.

> After the meeting in Oakland, someone had to actually write down the protocol and circulate it to the interested parties for their tacit approval. This process was rather informal.

HEFTER: It wasn't very rigorous in the standards-making process, but I think we still had a good consensus of manufacturers.[8]

LE: *How did you compare the process then, in terms of review, with the process you and the ESTA control protocols working group are undergoing in 1999–2000, to get the protocol adopted as an ANSI standard?*

HEFTER: It was not rigorous. It probably would not pass ANSI muster. We still hit on a lot of the manufacturers. We got a pretty good consensus. I think if we'd gone through a formal ANSI process at that time, the results would not have been a whole lot different.

TERRY: if you look at the new ESTA Technical Standards Program, we have a policy and procedures document that is forty pages long, and there is public review at every step of the way.

LE: *That's a good thing, and more in line with what other standards-making organizations do.*

TERRY: That carries with it a penalty, though. But it has to, for a trade organization, because the antitrust considerations are so strong. You can't be in a position where you are seen as favoring one company or another. The great success of the DMX512 standard—and its drawback—was that it came out fast, but in somewhat shoddy condition. It should have been a much more detailed document, but it was right out there for people to start implementing. Quickly, the interconnectivity thing just snowballed. Not only could we not get away with that today, we wouldn't want to. We know a lot more about standards making that we did in 1986. What did we know about standards then? Standards were something that somebody else wrote and that we had to follow.

---

8. DMX512 is currently undergoing a major revision through the ESTA Technical Standards Program, which uses a more codified ANSI standards adoption process.

FOSTER: No Ethernet protocol can be designed from the stage of a trade show by eight people and say, "We're done." It's just so much more complex than that. Nor can a standard evolve designed by a committee, which is again a big problem. Because there are particular needs, or there are so many technological decisions, which can go so many legitimately different ways, that to get the egos of engineers and different companies in alignment is really a challenge.

HEFTER: A comment we've been making at some of the recent meetings is that if we knew then what we know now, certain things would have been different. But we still had a pretty reasonable consensus of the manufacturers at that time. I remember for the 1990 revision we were definitely circulating it to thirty to forty manufacturers; it probably wasn't as many in '86.

TERRY: I'll go on to describe what happened after [the conference]. At that meeting everybody said "yeah, OK," and it was a very short meeting. Everybody said, "OK, we'll do that . . . who will do it?" Everybody looked around as if to say, "OK, who's been shooting their mouth off the loudest in this meeting?" That was me.

I came back to New York and I said, "I'm going to write this down and we're going to poll a few people who are right now actively interested in applying it." The most vocal people on what to do to modify the Colortran protocol were Steve Carlson, Gordon Pearlman's partner at Entertainment Technology, and Tim Burnham, then of ARRI, GB. Tim was developing a product called the Arri Connection, which was a multiplexer-demultiplexer system which would take in analog inputs, multiplex it onto digital data with the ability to patch, and there was a demultiplexer as well that would take that digital data and split it out to analog. They were right in the development cycle on this project, so they wanted us to do it [develop a standard digital protocol] because they wanted to adopt it right then. There was a lot of back and forth. The only really contentious issue was whether the thing should run at 153.6 kilobits per second, which was the Colortran rate, or the faster 250 kilobits per second, which it ended up being. Carlson argued that, first of all, it had to be a baud rate that could easily be generated from microcontrollers. To date, all of these digital multiplex schemes were hardware implementations. If you went to a Colortran dimmer pack, you didn't find a microprocessor in it. You found basically a hardware machine with a UART, a bunch of counters, a bunch of sample and hold amplifiers, but there was no processor there. The 153.6 kilobits per second was difficult to generate on many microprocessors because it wasn't divisible; using a 4-megahertz clock, it didn't divide down to get you 153.6. So we went back and forth, back and forth, what should we do; some people wanted slower, some people wanted faster. The rock and roll people wanted faster. Matt Deakin of Celco commented on the early standard, and actually he's responsible for the concept of alternate start codes. . . . He said we need faster because the rock and roll people thought that even 44 hertz, even 250 kilobits per second was pretty marginal, because when you're doing very fast chases, marquee chases, what you have is an effect where the update rate beats against the chase rate and you get artifacts in the chase; you don't have clean chases. So they said, "We have got to have more updates." Two hundred fifty kilobits per second at that point was totally stretching the ability of a lot of these hardware UARTs that were in the existing equipment. You had to practically hand select the UART to run at that 4-megahertz clock speed. So 250 was a real stretch. Some people said "more more more," and other people said "no, because we don't want to have to use processors. We want to be able to use readily available UARTs." So finally I said, "OK, enough discussion," in a very arbitrary way, in a way that would never possibly fly today. I said, "OK, here it is." Six or eight people reviewed it—I think we called it the gang of eight or something like that—everybody said, "OK, great," and we published it.

There were a few problems, to say the least. The first problem was the technical problem of "did it work?" If you take a manufacturer of dimmers and a manufacturer of consoles, hand them the standard, have them go off and do their thing, did the things talk to each other? Nooo way. Leaving that aside for a minute, I went on a one-man promotional tour to get the idea of the standard accepted. The first thing that happened was that the PLASA magazine, *Lighting and Sound International*, published a center spread tear-out of the standard, complete, which was a huge step. Then, Pat MacKay published the complete standard in both *Lighting Dimensions* and *Theatre Crafts*, another big step. Then I wrote to Len Auerbach, who was the president of the ASTC[9] at the time. I said,

---

9. American Society of Theatre Consultants.

"Listen, here's a wonderful new thing and here are all the reasons that you should do it." And he came back and said no way. He said, "We're not doing this, you can't tell us how to do it." It was a very antistandard, don't-tell-us-what-to-do kind of thing. So there was a lot of hostility from the consultants initially. To his credit, Len laughs about that now.

Then the manufacturers. Of course, at Production Arts, the day that we came out of that meeting, or rather the day that we set the 250 kilobits per second rate, we changed over all of our Lighting Methods dimming equipment and all of our consoles to deal with DMX512 and to produce that protocol. We were on board right away. Then, we were twisting the arms of the other rental shops to come aboard. Everyone had been really vocal, but when it came to spending some money to actually convert, people were saying, "Hmm, do we really need to do this?" So, Vanco stayed on the Micro II protocol, which was the proprietary LMI protocol, for years after DMX showed up. We sort of drove the bandwagon. Interestingly enough, Kliegl didn't get on board. Gordon Pearlman [whose company Entertainment Technology was consulting with Kliegl] had been right out there saying, "Look, this is the standard we need." But then after it was available, Kliegl went right on still shipping their same old proprietary K96 protocol and it took a long time. Because then there were a lot of people saying, "This standard is a piece of crap. Look, it has no error checking, it is not fast enough, it's technically a bad piece of work." That went on for years. Practically from '86 to '90, all we heard was how bad the standard was.

> Nevertheless, Steve Terry forged ahead, leading a Control Communications Standards Committee within USITT. This committee set out to develop controller-to-controller communications. The committee also started working on something they called in 1987 the "advanced peripheral communication standard." According to a published article written by Steve Terry, "This standard will specifically address the needs of the automated fixtures and other advanced peripherals which will be used by the entertainment industry during the next decade."[10] Thirteen years later, the ESTA Technical Standards Program is working on something now called ACN, Advanced Control Network.

---

10. Terry, Steve. "Entertainment Industry Standards: USITT Committee Considers Control Communications," *Lighting Dimensions*, January/February 1987, p. 90.

TERRY: Let's go back for a minute to the mistakes that we made in the standard originally. Because we all knew what the standard was, we understood it very clearly, we did not provide a lot of exposition in the standard about how to make interoperability happen and what the worst-case issues for timing would be. One of the most amazing things about the standard is that there are timing parameters, where it says "minimum 4 microseconds, maximum 1 second, typical none." Well, why was that? Because we were absolutely scared that if we put a standard out there that was too onerous, no manufacturer would adopt it. So we said, "OK, we're going to put a standard out there that has such wide tolerance, such wide windows, that nobody can argue about adopting it." But that created the interoperability problem. That problem is better now.

HEFTER: Some of the concerns about the reliability or the precision of the standards didn't always manifest themselves—the comments about both AMX192 and DMX512 not being good because there is no error checking, for example. Of course, AMX192 being analog, there is more chance of noise issues. In some installations that may have been true, but I think that, with the amount of it out there, obviously there are some places where noise may have been an issue, but for the vast majority of stuff out there, I don't think it was as big an issue as some people would say. Of course, being in a manufacturing position, I wouldn't necessarily hear all these issues.

FLORAC: There was a DMX 1990, but before that, right after DMX originally got approved, I went to Dallas. There were a bunch of people who sat in a meeting and tried to establish the next one. We started looking at another protocol called the EBU, which is a protocol that the television and film industry used—still use—to talk between equipment. We were trying to add some more intelligence to the protocol because the original DMX protocol, though it has a minor amount of error checking, was basically a hardware protocol. It defines the copper; it defines, in essence, the hardware at the end you need to communicate to it. The language itself that it talks over the wires is really, really simple, and over the years various things have been used and adopted. It's kind of like Ethernet. When you have Ethernet, you can have two pieces on Ethernet but you can't have a Novell server just start talking to a Microsoft server. Even though they're both Ethernet, they're both not talking the same language because they were developed differently, even though they're both on the same platform. . . . What happens if we put this intelligence in here and someone puts it on a pyro device and there's a fire, and somebody dies—are we liable as an organization?

We made a few flaws in the standard on the first time through but fixed most of them in 1990. There were some timing issues that were not considered. We made the mistake of assuming that everybody was going to do what we [at LMI] were doing. And they took the standard and said, "Well, if it doesn't say I can't do this, that means I can." We didn't put enough information into the standard to pull people to go with the flow. We wanted them to go with the flow, but unless you put that in writing, they didn't. So they often did various things that didn't work and you'd start getting DMX protocols that didn't work with each other, for a short period of time. It was a minor amount of hell. The combinations that didn't work with LMI were pretty minimal. We had some problems with Colortran at one time and fixed those right away. We had interpreted the standard very liberally and made ourselves deal with that. We also had enough port power on the receiving side to handle any combination. We were already in the business of building interface boxes for anybody to go with anybody else. So I had already been interfacing between Colortran equipment, whose protocol at the time varied between consoles. Say a protocol had four different consoles talking four different ways. So we'd already learned to adapt to about anything, so that was not a problem for LMI in general. At the time we didn't make anything that transmitted, so that wasn't an issue. Some of the small guys didn't quite catch onto it . . . they tried to take a little processor and . . . didn't quite have the horsepower to deal with it.

TERRY: We revised DMX512 in 1990, and actually that project was led by Michael Callahan. Michael took charge of the administrative aspects of it. It was the gang of eight again: Bob Goddard, Michael Callahan, Bill Florac—I don't know if he was at LMI or ETC; he probably was with LMI at that point—Steve Carlson at Entertainment Technology. We went and we cleaned it up. First of all we cleaned up a kind of basic mistake, which was that we specified, inadvertently, a timing parameter called "mark after break" which was at 4 microseconds, and none of the hardware UARTs or processors could come out of that break and start dealing with data in less than 4 microseconds. So we widened that parameter. And we added explanations and a better timing diagram, and we tried to make the thing easier to understand.

LE: *But were you still saying that this protocol is just for consoles talking to dimmers?*

TERRY: Absolutely. That's all it was. Even in 1990 that's all it was.

> Despite Steve Terry's comment in 1997, in 1987 he had written, as noted earlier, of developing an "advanced peripheral communication standard" to address the automated light issue. This was to have been a separate communication standard from DMX512. No one could foresee how the DMX512 standard would be used.

HEFTER: It was always thought DMX512 would be sort of an option. . . . Everyone would use their own standard protocol, their proprietary protocol, but when you have that instance where you need to get someone else's console to run your stuff, then you switch over to DMX. It's like the roadhouse situation. The rental companies were very interested in the process. Nobody expected that it would take off the way it did. The concept of the distribution amplifier for DMX was not even in our mindset.[11] You plug it in the booth, you wire a dimmer rack onstage or underneath the stage or wherever, and that was it.

FLORAC: I think that we didn't have enough foresight to realize . . . it needed to be a better protocol. It makes a fine dimming protocol. It's only error checking that's repetitive. When you start getting into moving lights, or start burning pyro or something like that, a more secure, robust network is important, and we weren't able to accomplish that. Mostly because we wanted the manufacturers to adopt this right away, and the only way to do that was to use this platform. Probably the high-

---

11. As DMX512 became more widely used, engineers soon realized that a device would be necessary to split, amplify, and optically isolate the digital signal if it were going to different types of devices.

est technology on the market at the time was Avab. They had a bidirectional, very intelligent protocol which we looked at and said, "Nah, we don't want to do this." Every time we started heading that direction we started getting into areas we didn't want to go into because if we did, we would never finish the protocol. . . .

HEFTER: I remember getting the drawings and stuff and creating the CAD drawings. At that time it was all cut and paste . . . doing all the formatting and stuff at Strand, and then getting it to the national office [of USITT] for them to print up. And when we did the revision—at that time I was at Macro Electronics—I did the same thing there. I might have actually done that on my home computer at that time. I actually had one at that point. And I remember we had a problem with it. I had actually sent it to them on disk at one point, and wherever they sent it out to print, couldn't deal with the mu character [μ] for "microsecond." So there were actually a number of copies that were distributed that had microseconds reading as seconds in some of the diagrams. Not good. We had a little problem with that. We think we've got that issue resolved now. The next time I sent them a hard copy. I'm still essentially the source; if they need to reprint, they check with me.

FLORAC: [In 1990 there was] an attempt to do a DMX test box so they could test everybody's DMX against the standard and see if it really worked or not. I don't think that was a bad idea after all. . . .

LE TO FRED FOSTER: *At the original meeting in 1986, is it true that no one really thought of this as anything but a way to talk to dimmers?*

FOSTER: I don't think that's so. Maybe not at that meeting, but it certainly came out before it was done: the ability to have start codes, because we all wanted to be able to do different things. Our particular architecture of downloading the patch, we wanted a way to be able to do that. So there were provisions such as the whole alternate start code idea, but to my knowledge nobody's really exploited that for the purpose of having proprietary data on it. I think that the Rosco feedback method uses it. But back in 1985, there certainly was no representation in that group by wiggle light companies. There functionally were no wiggle light companies other than Vari-Lite. There was Moto-Lights or whatever their name was, and they were just analog.[12] So it hadn't become a big need and it certainly wasn't conceived of, to my recollection.

HEFTER: But the direction it took off nobody expected; same thing with the whole motion control, intelligent fixtures, moving lights area. We saw something like that may be happening; those things were just starting to happen. Of course the Vari-Lites were around for a while at that point, and others were starting to appear. That's one of the reasons the alternate start code concept was adopted.

LE TO BRAD RODRIGUEZ: *When you and this whole group of people were originally working with this in the mid '80s, did you anticipate the impact it had vis-à-vis automation and how accessible it made automated lights, and how the automated light manufacturers just picked up on it?*

RODRIGUEZ: Well, I sure didn't [laughter]. I don't know about the other people on the committee, but it's been going in places we never envisioned, or I certainly never envisioned. We didn't think of it in the context of automated fixtures.

LE: *You were just thinking dimmers . . .*

RODRIGUEZ: It's ironic in that Strand was looking at automated fixtures at the time, but we thought they'd have their own separate control protocol.

LE: *And did they? Did Strand develop anything for the American market?*

RODRIGUEZ: No, other than I think they had color changers; that is all they actually wound up developing. There was a small outfit, whose name I can't remember, which was only a few miles away from Strand that was doing these things on a semicustom basis. They had some actually fairly clever fixtures, and they had their own control protocol. I know Strand looked at acquiring that technology, but other than getting their color changer I don't know that Strand ever did. Their technology turned out to have some mechanical problems that of course I, the software person, would not have noticed.

---

12. Moto-Lights were made by Morpheus.

LE: *And of course in DMX there are some problems running automated lights. You seemed to have done a lot of work on enhancements to the original DMX protocol?*

RODRIGUEZ: I actually wrote a proposal for enhanced DMX.

LE: *Where did that go?*

RODRIGUEZ: Nowhere. . . . When I was still attending the USITT conference I did circulate that. They were having these annual DMX sessions. There was 512A, which was to rectify one—in retrospect—really stupid mistake that was left in the protocol, which was that one timing parameter was specified tightly that didn't need to be specified tightly. There was no need for it to be exactly 8 microseconds, but that's how it got written—512A loosened that up. Doug Fleenor, who at the time was with Teatronics, and I kicked around a lot of ideas for expanding DMX512, and he and I put together what was going to be the bidirectional DMX512, which would let the dimmers talk back to the console. At this time, in the early '90s, there was starting to be more interest in smart dimmers—dimmers that could send information back, having a two-way communication. I think that we brought that out for consideration at the same USITT conference that Strand brought out the SMX protocol. I believe that was at Calgary. It might have been a meeting or two after that Calgary conference. But nothing ever came of it. We put it out there. We said, "Look, this is what we're thinking about. If people are interested in it let's take it to the next stage." But it just sort of sat there.

LE: *Do you think it didn't go anywhere because manufacturers are interested in keeping the feedback proprietary?*

RODRIGUEZ: No. Actually, when we first brought that out, what we got from many manufacturers was "we're still coping with DMX512 manure and we're not ready to go to the next stage yet." Bidirectional DMX512 would, of necessity, be something of a hack, because DMX512 wasn't originally designed to be a bidirectional protocol. It was designed to have one transmitter and many receivers. And while we came up with some lovely backward-compatible clever inventions that would make it possible to use all DMX equipment on this protocol, I suspect there was an attitude of, "Well, this is the time to start with a clean sheet of paper. Design a new protocol that overcomes the limitations and is designed for this from the beginning." In fact, I think some of us were looking at SMX. I know when Strand bought out the SMX protocol I started designing all my hardware to be SMX-capable. I don't know whatever happened to SMX, by the way. You have to realize that it was only a year or two later that I left the lighting industry. It hadn't been adopted at the time, by anyone except Strand, by the time I left the industry. Whatever did become of it? Is it in wide use today?

LE: *No. Not at all.*

RODRIGUEZ: Didn't get anywhere either?

LE: *It got put out in the public domain, and from what I understand, even though it was in the public domain, there's some legal rigmarole about it being in the public domain, but you can't use it without licensing it from Strand.*

RODRIGUEZ: Oh, yeah. Well, I've seen weird licensing like that before.

LE: *And because of that, according to one person who's a competing manufacturer, because of that it's not in wide use.*

> Despite the fact that DMX512 is not a bidirectional protocol, there was some room for expansion in the use of it as a protocol for controlling devices other than dimmers. The standard specifies certain "start codes," which Foster and Hefter referred to earlier. A "start code" is that part of the control signal that tells the device what type of signal is to follow. For example, a null start following a reset is the default value and indicates that the information to follow is dimmer level information. Provision is made in the standard for up to 255 additional start codes. At the time of the 1990 revision, there was some discussion about maintaining a start code registry.

HEFTER: Steve Terry and I have been keeping up the start code list. He essentially has a piece of paper in his drawer, and I have a file on the computer, and when things have come up on the start code, then he and I talk.

FLORAC: We had enough foresight to put in the start code. We thought that we could have one code for this, one code for that . . . zero was dimming, one for moving lights or . . . moving lights weren't invented at the time but we wanted to have expansion to it.

LE: *Nobody used the alternate start codes—is that true?*

HEFTER: Very few people used it. . . . Most of the intelligent fixture people totally ignored a couple things in the standard. One was that the alternate start code was meant to deal with things like that. Start code zero was supposed to be just dimmers.

> In 1992, USITT, jointly with PLASA, published "DMX512: A Guide for Users and Installers," by Adam Bennette. This guide provided practical information beyond just the actual timing diagrams provided in the written standard.

TERRY: This book is actually the definitive document. It started out as six pages and after the committee finished with it, it was eighty pages. It's sort of amazing. What we did was take Adam's document, which he was going to sell for PLASA. He wanted to make money off the publication. We all got together and convinced him he should sell it for a nominal one-time fee, put it in the hands of the committee, and subject it to some review. First of all, this would never have happened but for Adam, because like all standards works, one person has to have the passion to make it happen. He did a ton of work on this. And we were unmerciful with him in the review process. The group (Steve Carlson from ETI, Bill Florac from ETC, Bob Goddard, Philip Nye from DHA, Gary Pritchard from LSC in Australia, and myself, Ralph Weber, a bunch of people), went through the document and we said, "Adam, this book is not called 'Uncle Adam tells you what you can get away with using DMX512.' You have to take some of this stuff out." He said, "Well, what do you mean? You *can* get away with this." We said, "Yeah, if it says you can, then people will." So we did a lot of work on making it not "what you can get away with" but "how to do it right." We go into absolutely the right way to do it. And it's the definitive document.

> The DMX512 standard specifies the use of five-pin connectors to accommodate two pairs of data wire and a ground. One of the things manufacturers—moving light manufacturers especially—

have been "able to get away with" is the use of three-pin connectors and only one data pair.

HEFTER: A lot of moving light manufacturers use three-pin XLR connectors.[13] This may have been a savings to them, but it's been a great cost to the users and the dealers. It was interesting sitting in the ESTA meetings and seeing a couple of the people hear this. And there was a little bit of amazement on their faces that this was as big an issue as we all see it is.

LE: *You're talking about the recent meetings at which further revision of DMX512 is being discussed?*

HEFTER: Yes, current meetings.

LE: *I assume you now have moving light manufacturers represented?*

HEFTER: Right. One manufacturer said the engineers knew this was wrong [to use three-pin connectors]. They say their PC boards are designed to take a five-pin XLR, once they can get management to go with it. They actually have that design in place, but they still, because management wants to use the three-pin for cost containment, still do it; yet they say the conversion would be very easy. You're talking about a couple of bucks a connector, versus having to go buy two in-line connectors and cable and labor and the hassle. The cost to the fixture—that is, the end cost to the consumer—is going to be a lot less if they'd just put the five pins in to start with.

LE: *In your role as USITT engineering commissioner, did you get feedback from end users at all on the original standard? Feedback from consultants and dealers?*

HEFTER: I don't recall receiving any, particularly. Once we were all done, we were kind of amazed that it happened. But I think obviously that it's been good for the industry. I think the fears that we were sensing from the sales/marketing types were unfounded. I think it's allowed the industry to grow.

---

13. The DMX512 standard calls for five-pin connectors where pin 1 is signal ground, pin 2 is data–, pin 3 is data+, pin 4 spare data–, and pin 5 spare data+.

<u>LE:</u> *Well, it certainly has made—and this is why I'm focusing on this event—it certainly made automation accessible. Which it hadn't been before. In one sense, automation didn't really exist in the "legitimate" theatre because there was no standard control, and what did exist was inaccessible to the normal theatrical user. DMX really made it possible to use automated lights within a conventional rig.*

<u>HEFTER:</u> I guess the one concern I've had about it is there's probably been some inappropriate uses of DMX. Some people have been using it to do things like pyro or lasers. . . . There's this one laser organization that almost talks about DMX as if it was theirs.

<u>LE:</u> *And you say it's inappropriate because there are safety issues involved?*

<u>HEFTER:</u> You don't have the talkback, so there are cases where, unless there are other safeties built into the laser equipment itself, that this may not be appropriate. And in fact, some of this is being discussed in the proposed revisions. There are proposals addressing places where DMX may not be appropriate. And so there's concern about that; that some people have taken it too far. The other thing about being accessible, one of the things that's happening with ACN [Advanced Control Network] is that, because that's such a big methodological step—much more than DMX is—the intent is to make a basic developer's package available so the small companies can still get on board and be able to deal with it. Many may simply choose to just do an ACN-to-DMX converter. DMX won't go away. Just as 0 to 10 volts [analog signal] is still out there, DMX is not going to go away for a long time either. And so there are efforts being made on ACN to make sure that some of the smaller players that don't have the resources don't get left behind.

<u>FOSTER:</u> The standard has certainly affected how theaters are designed. We're seeing, at least with some consultants, the front-of-house transfer panel with its cord patch unplugging 2P+G[14] and plugging into the roadrack, going away and being replaced by a DMX port that you plug the touring board into. So all of those things are positive arguments for standardization. Negative arguments for it, and a limitation on stan-

---

14. "2P+G" or "2 pin + ground" connectors are standard stage connectors for carrying 20-amp load circuits.

dardization, something that slows it down, is that once you have a standard, it gains momentum, and somebody who takes their product development off of that standard path is taking a risk to do that. There's a reason that we did it, because we had to do remote video and we had to build these control systems that were very diverse. But we're investing a lot of money to do that. We want to be there first, we want to capitalize on it for a while, and so that is an argument against it. And we want to be exclusive. And so it's been an interesting change to have played on both sides of the commercial argument, and then look back to say what is the best place for it to end up.

LE TO STEVE TERRY: *Do you think standardized protocols have been good for the industry?*

TERRY: Oh, yes. It has created tens of millions of dollars of revenue, which ultimately get pumped backed into research and development, in the development of new products that are made available to the design community. I think if it hadn't been DMX512, it would have been something else that got forced into the same mold.

FOSTER: I do still believe that the standard helped the industry; it helped the manufacturers. I probably don't share Steve's pure vision that it helped everybody. The plug-and-play nature that it gave to the industry was invaluable to the industry, and it was the right thing to do for our customers. And of course that's the right thing for us to do. But from a commercial standpoint, it did undermine the monolithic structure; it fractured any full-range manufacturer's product line and control of a project.

LE: *Have there been any adverse affects vis-à-vis quality control because it is such an open architecture? Are there third-party or second-class developers putting out second-rate products that wouldn't have been possible without this standard?*

TERRY: Yeah, you bet. And the market decides.

HEFTER: Yes. That's absolutely true.

SECTION 4

What Changes We Have Wrought: The Effects of Computer Control and Automation

As I sat watching *Angels in America* in 1994, I was astounded by its fluidity. This plasticity, I suspected, resulted not only from Tony Kushner's fine use of language, but from the exploitation of contemporary stagecraft by set designer Robin Wagner and lighting designer Jules Fisher. Yet, the relationship of contemporary stagecraft to contemporary playwrighting poses something of a "chicken and egg" question. Have changing theatrical forms driven the research and development that resulted in the LS-8 and Light Palette? Or have playwrights been freed by technology to write as fluidly for the stage as they do for film? There is, of course, no single answer. Rather, there is a web of response and opinion about this question and others. Digital technologies have affected the lighting design process, lighting design organization, lighting design pedagogy, and, some would argue, negatively affected lighting design quality.

LE: *There is so much more flexibility in lighting control now than there was twenty years ago. Do you think that has changed the kind of theatre that we are seeing?*

NEIL PETER JAMPOLIS: I think it has changed the kind of theatre. I think that the thinking in theatre was certainly moving toward the "cinematic" ahead of the lighting being able to do those kinds of effects, but I think that the advances in lighting have accelerated that process. So maybe it's a baby chicken, and then a big egg. It is so possible to make instantaneous and complete changes of look with so little effort. The effort wasn't ever in the writing of a cue. You can always write the look. It was the refining it and the going back. This kind of accelerated, cinematic theatre of movement, where the lights are choreographed as much as any dancers or actors, is really being unleashed through the possibilities of the technology. The real nightmare has always been when there was a train wreck of some sort with the cues, and one had to get back to where you were before it happened. This would consume many minutes, sometimes longer; where people would have to go back to the last blackout and track their every move—and so you would not do it because it wasn't worth the trouble.

LE TO KEN BILLINGTON: *You have talked about how shows have gotten really big. It's fairly obvious; a show has 1,200 lights and 700 or 800 dimmers. Do you think that all of that new stuff and the quantity of it have changed the form of theatre today?*

KEN BILLINGTON: I don't know if it has changed the form. What has happened is that shows are brighter. They are much brighter than they were. I think that the public demands that. So I think a lot of that has gone into the intensity for performing, especially from the front. I remember I was doing some show when Lee Watson[1] used to write his reviews, and he took me to task because I had forty to sixty—maybe it was seventy some-odd lamps on the box booms. He thought just twelve would be enough. He took me to task because there were seventy. Well you know now, if I can get away with doing a Broadway show with less than 150 lights out front, the response today would be "look what they did." So there it is brighter by default. I think it is probably more sophisticated—there are more subtle changes. I'm not saying they're good or bad, it's just you can have anything you want. There are probably a lot more templates and gobos on the stage than anybody had ever even thought of. I remember back in the '70s, if I wanted a gobo, I hired someone to cut them out of pie plates. And then Joe Tawil, when he was running Colortran, came out with eighteen templates and it was like

1. Throughout the 1970s and into the '80s, Lee Watson, now deceased, wrote reviews of the lighting of primarily Broadway shows for *Lighting Dimensions* magazine.

this revelation. Gobos: Jo Mielziner had designed them years earlier and they were in brass, were just holes burnt through the brass. Pie plates were better, but you didn't get very sophisticated leaf templates. So gobos were almost nonexistent until this little stock item that Colortran came out with. And it made life easier, but then you had to order lights that had gobo holders because not every light had a gobo holder. So if you had a spare hung and you said, "OK, let's put a leaf in here," they probably had to take the light down and call the shop and get one that was designed to take gobos. That was an extra when you ordered a spotlight, the gobo holder.

MITCH DANA: Most of the plays that I do now, or most of the shows that I do now, are complicated shows. And they require more. I think it would have been much more difficult to have done a *Philadelphia, Here I Come* back then than it is now. First of all, you couldn't have lit it the same way and had the two worlds coexist in the same space at the same time. But now with computer boards you can write the 250 cues that are necessary to keep one person in one world and follow him around the stage anywhere he goes and keep him separate from the world everybody else is in. I don't think that could have been done, certainly not easily, back in the '70s.

DENNIS PARICHY: We think about lighting in more complex ways now just because we *can* do more. It's so easy to do these things; we're now exploring things we would have never attempted before. I think that's the main difference. I can't say I'm up on what all my fellow designers have been doing around the country or even in New York; as usual, you're busy doing your own shows and you don't see a lot of what other people do. But in general I feel that everyone is trying to do more with lighting than ever before. And I notice the young guys whom I encounter and the students I teach, they want to go haywire—they want to throw moving lights in on everything. They think of it as unlimited numbers of dimmers, whereas I still tend to think of it as "what are our limitations here?" And they seem to come at it more as if there aren't really any limitations—until someone says, "You can't afford that." Whereas, I had a tendency to start with, "Well, in this circumstance, what are my limitations of time, money, equipment?" Then I'll figure out what I'm going to do.

JEFF DAVIS: My take on it is not that people are aware of lighting. I think that people are so influenced by movies and cinematography, that the young playwrights are basically people who grew up watching film, not live theatre. You get the playwrights like . . . the interesting ones like Terence McNally and . . . the older crowd, Kander and Ebb, those people that really do write for the theater and understand it. But I think a lot of people basically are influenced by film, and say, "We'll just do a quick cut to this." Then it becomes the scene designer and the lighting designer's problem. . . . About the same time that we were getting the technology to do computer boards, we were getting this generation of people that basically were writing movies for the stage. I can't believe . . . at least in my experience it's hard to find a director that's lighting-knowledgeable, let alone a playwright [laughter]. So I can't believe that [lighting technology] had any influence on anybody writing the show.

LE: *Do you think that lighting itself is functioning differently now than it did twenty years ago?*

DAVIS: Absolutely. It seems to me that in the old days, the emphasis was not on technical theatre. Not only were you doing lighting control with piano boards, you didn't have all the electronic control to do winches and fly systems and all that other stuff that everybody is now using. I think that the producers are also very influenced and afraid of things like MTV. It seems to me that on Broadway there's an attitude that if you don't change it and bang it around every thirty seconds, it'll bore the hell out of the audience. I basically am of the opinion that if it bores you when you read it, if it bores you in rehearsal, no matter how much other stuff you do, it's going to bore you in the theatre.

If you're not interested in the story, it doesn't matter how much stuff you throw around it. It might sell tickets, but I don't think it actually makes good theatre. The shows that are good are the ones where the plot rivets you. Not to negate what we do, in supporting that. My old joke is, "You're much better off going to *Cats* and watching the dimmer check." There, we have . . . a show. What they're doing on stage doesn't interest me, particularly. That's my own opinion; it obviously interests a lot of other people, because it's still on.

LE: *Well, it's ironic, because this past week* Cats *became the longest-running show ever, surpassing* A Chorus Line, *which is the example of a very simply but specifically designed show that had wonderful lighting.*

DAVIS: Right, and the lighting was as much choreography as the choreography. It's interesting to me that despite all the technology—and this tells you what my aesthetic taste is—but I still think that one of the best-looking, best-lit shows, best-designed shows ever done was *Follies.* You look at those Sondheim musicals: *Follies, Company, Night Music, Pacific Overtures,* all of those shows that were done on piano boards, done by Tharon Musser, in a great collaboration with Hal Prince and Boris Aronson. There have not been many shows that have knocked my socks off like those did, as visual experiences . . . and obviously *Chorus Line* . . . and maybe *Grand Hotel* was that impeccably done. With all this technology, is lighting any better? I don't know. It's all craft and technology. I'm not sure the art of it is any better than what people did on piano boards.

LE TO BILL WARFEL: *Do you think that the flexibility that was made available by computer control has changed the kinds of plays and musicals we're seeing produced today?*

BILL WARFEL: I think it has changed the way we see them.

LE: *What do you mean by that?*

WARFEL: It's a funny kind of evolution. It's a funny kind of codependence with the concert world. When rock music started being performed in the precursors of today's concerts, they had all sorts of light effects. Because there wasn't anything else to look at, light effects worked, and people loved it, so the concert world got into this business of light effects. And a generation, almost two generations, grew up with that sort of awareness of the possibilities of light effects, which don't necessarily relate to the plays, but it's there in the background. Now along come these boards where it's possible to do things that we had to do manually before so you couldn't really realize them. Now along comes the possibility of doing them automatically and therefore they can happen: "Oh gosh, this thing will do a double chase at variable speed while there's a slow fade going on using inhibitive submasters. Wow, let's do it!" That kind of feeling was there. So OK, we do it. I don't think that has had a tremendous impact on plays, but it's had just an incredible impact on musicals. We went from steady-state thinking, which is a dynamic move from this look to that look; we stay in that steady state until it makes sense to have a dynamic move to another one. (I will die as a steady-state thinker.) We went from that to having light that's almost constantly moving in most musicals, along with the musical. Now, you don't see this in plays. That goes back to the influence of the concert world, which was a very mobile, fluid, constantly changing thing. And now it's possible for the boards to do this, and there are people who can conceive of it and keep it in their heads, God bless them, so it happens. And in the big musicals there's a convergence between concert lighting and lighting for musicals. Now that there are movable lights, that convergence is coming even faster.

CURT OSTERMANN: I've been away from musicals for so long, and I don't do plays any more. I'm mostly doing television and industrial theatre. But I think that the fact that most of the Broadway musicals lately have been huge production things, I think that has an effect on the lighting design. And I'm very biased against those kinds of shows. I think if you have a great book and great actors and singers and dancers, you don't need to do anything except help it along. And a lot of times I find that the design *is* the show, and there's no book, and there's no really great talent up there. I always go back to *Chorus Line*. There were, I think, less than three hundred lights; maybe a little more than two hundred units. And a black box set that went to mirrors every once in a while, and that show was fabulous, because it was written well.

LE: *And* A Chorus Line *used only ninety-six dimmers.*

OSTERMANN: Right. Only seventy-two on the bus-and-truck. I did that show with Tharon. I did the bus-and-truck and a couple of the national companies [as assistant lighting designer]. For me, it was the best lighting on Broadway, and it used very few units, compared to what there are now. So, yes, I think computers have changed the style of production.

STEVE TERRY: I find the change in scale really startling. I will never forget, when the LS-8 came out, it was 96 dimmers. There were 134 cues in that show; actually, I was reading a book about *Chorus Line* where Tharon said it was 134 cues. And man, I was there every night running those cues, so I knew there were a lot of them. And it was a complicated show and I thought, when I read this: "One hundred thirty-four cues, that's a joke, that's like the first five minutes of a show today." This whole issue of 96 dimmers—96 dimmers was considered mind-boggling. They blew the Kliegl Performer out to 125 channels, wow! It was unheard of that you'd need 125 channels.

LE: *It's similar to the discussions when DMX came out when people said, "Who's going to need 512 channels on a show?"*

TERRY: Yes, well, at twenty-five per moving light you use them up . . .

OSTERMANN: I think there is too much lighting going on on Broadway right now. I think that we're trapped in big production, too much scenery, too much lighting, too many costumes, and not enough substance. I feel that as designers we're always there to help but we should never dominate—or almost never dominate.

LE: *What about a show that is conceived to be an effects show, like Vegas shows such as* EFX *or* Siegried and Roy?

OSTERMANN: Right. But that's something else again. Las Vegas is different. I think too much of that has happened to Broadway. Broadway used to be the testing grounds for people like Tennessee Williams. And now no one will produce plays any more because they won't make enough money doing it. And not enough audience members want to go see it. And I think that's a problem—or maybe we're assuming that. It's not a problem in Chicago. It seems like they've got awfully good theatre going on in Chicago. And good playwrights; Steppenwolf Theatre is doing great stuff there. And Broadway I think is just too expensive now to become experimental again.

Shortly after this interview was conducted, Tennesee Williams' 1938 play *Not About Nightingales* had its world premiere at Circle in the Square Theatre in New York. This production of a "lost" Williams play was directed by Trevor Nunn and originally produced at London's National Theatre and Houston's Alley Theatre.

The lighting design was by Chris Parry, who was nominated for a Tony award for his work on the show. There have been a number of other serious dramatic transplants from London in the intervening years, including Yasmina Reza's *Art* and Michael Frayn's *Copenhagen.* Whereas in the late 1970s to 1990s many decried the preponderance of British megamusicals on the Broadway stage, few are complaining about these more recent dramas, often produced in conjunction with American producers or, in the case of *Not About Nightingales,* American not-for-profit theatres.

As Curt Ostermann implied, the design process—and the design goals—of a Vegas extravaganza differ from that of a straight play. I asked Natasha Katz to discuss that process especially with regard to the use of emerging technologies.

LE: *How were the aesthetic goals of* EFX *communicated to you? How did they develop?*

NATASHA KATZ: The paradox of *EFX* in a certain sense is that, although it's true the show is called *EFX*—I was thinking about this after you sent the fax—the effect we were hoping for was that we didn't want the lights to be flashing all the time. . . . What we were all hoping to do as a group, which is to say the director and the scenic designer and the choreographer, was to at least understand that the effects had to come from something. That's not to say that there was a great book for the show, because if anything that's its biggest downfall. But that you're more surprised by an effect when it's in some sort of context . . . whether it's . . . in the big scene in the show about Houdini. So at least in that particular case, effects are in the context of something else. It's not an effect for the sake of an effect. And that was really the goal of everybody, including Michael Crawford, that the show would somehow be grounded, and not just be effect after effect after effect. David Copperfield actually does a good job at that. It's all sort of story-based, and then all of a sudden you're transported into some "Oh my God, I can't believe that he did that" place. And that was what we were trying to do.

LE: *Did you develop some sort of visual through-line in the lighting to help do that, to help with the storytelling?*

KATZ: The other factor was that everybody who worked on the show were all Broadway people. Broadway only knows text. What I mean by that is that everything is so driven by the story when you're working on Broadway. And in Las Vegas, things are just driven. There's no rhyme or reason for it, in many cases. So . . . in terms of a conceptual through-line . . . the show is seven different scenes all pulled together by this effects master, this one person who is Michael Crawford. He says, "I'm the effects master and I'm going to show you this effect and that effect and that effect." So in truth it's a disparate show; it's seven completely different scenes tied together by one person. So if I were to ask "Is there a [visual through-line]?" . . . I would say, "No." Each scene was so entirely different, which was part of the point.

LE: *I'm sure scenically they are different, very different. How did you help to differentiate them scene by scene if that was part of the goal?*

KATZ: The first scene is about Merlin and it takes place on a mountaintop. And it was extremely idyllic and the lighting was, well, there were a lot of moving lights, but they were stationary through most of that scene, with a lot of gobos. So that it had a kind of happy, in the woods, kind of dappled, lighthearted look; the costumes were all light greens. And then in the middle of the scene a dragon appears. So it gets stormy, and fiery, so it's sort of like beautiful comedy turns to tragedy in a way. And then there were a lot of projections in the show.

Although perfectly appropriate for a Vegas extravaganza like *EFX*, using hundreds of lights and the most sophisticated control system for conventional and automated lights does not necessarily make for good design. Many people commented on the need to maintain design integrity in the face of almost infinite design possibilities.

LE TO STEVE TERRY: *There seems to be a generation of lighting designers who are reluctant to use technology or who view the gizmoization that's making lighting design more technically complicated not necessarily as a good thing.*

TERRY: It's created legions of bad lighting designers. Or it has encouraged what Tharon Musser calls the supermarket school of lighting . . .

LE: *Hang seven hundred lights, and then decide what it looks like.*

TERRY: That's exactly right. The fact that you can put a light anywhere and have it be any color, and hang seven hundred of them, is bad news. The problem is that the training levels on dealing with all of this equipment are nonexistent now. I have to tell you, ugly lighting with a thousand lights is a lot uglier than with 135 lights, because it gets right in your face. I won't name shows or name designers, because that would be rude and I would be killed. But there are a lot of designers out there who mask their fundamental lack of skill with a lot of very fancy equipment. But good for the industry, certainly. Good for the design process, do shows look better? They're brighter. They have a lot more flash, but . . . I remember going to see . . . Glenn Close and Jeremy Irons.

LE: The Real Thing.

TERRY: Maybe it was 1983 here in New York. It had a bazillion sets. Every time you turned around, the thing was going to a new set. Tharon lit that show with 135 lights, and it was some of the best lighting I ever saw in my life. And we were on that curve already, about hanging more, more, more. It was like "How big is yours?" "Well, mine is five hundred lights." So, it hasn't gotten better. But I don't think the DMX standard is necessarily the culprit here. You know, I think it's . . . the technology overall, but DMX was certainly an enabler.

BILLINGTON: What the computer console did was it freed us—we could put the lights at any level we wanted, we could cross-fade from anything we want to anything we want and cues became more—I don't want to say delicate or polished but—they became exactly what you wanted to paint the picture. If you just needed that down a half point, you could do it. Though I still to this day don't do it very much, I can. The capability is there if the sconces are too bright at 35, to put them at 32. If they're too bright at 32, put them at 28. Oh, 29 is better. So you can do that where you never could have done that before. So that's the great way that it's helped make the cues look better.

LE: *Is there a downside to that?*

BILLINGTON: I think the downside is lighting has a tendency to get now, because of computer control, a bit into, I like to say, "supermarket sweep." We can hang a light every eighteen inches wherever we have space. And we can plug it into its own dimmer. And we don't have to think about the cues. I still do because I come from an era when I had to design that way. Today, you know that you're going to use your area lights, you know you're going to use your backlights, but you don't have to worry about operation. You don't literally have to design the show in your head cue-wise now, so you can just hang the lights and if the director says, "Oh, we need something over there," you perhaps don't fight him, saying, "No, that isn't what we thought about" or "Why are we putting a light there?" You say, "OK, sure," and you focus something and turn it on. And even though you may not agree with it, you probably might give in to it. So I think now we can hang so much equipment and with the electronic peripherals from color changers to gobo changers to moving lights to name all the other stuff we can plug into this console to make it so we really don't ever have to make a decision of what color, which gobo, or where the light's going to be focused. We can make that decision on the fly. The shows have become very big and somewhat complicated. What we did when I used to do a musical on piano boards was that I had three electricians that were under contract that toured with the show or were part of the show or ran the lighting every night, as well as a follow spot operator, and perhaps a deck operator. By going to a memory board, I need only one man now. And we have tripled the amount of equipment. In the '60s and '70s, 350 to 400 lights was a big musical. A big musical now is 1,200 to 1,300 lights.

LE: *You said earlier that you used 42 dimmers on* Side by Side by Sondheim. *I'm wondering when was the last time you used 42 dimmers on a show.*

BILLINGTON: Boy, I'd love to again. Especially on a musical revue. I look back to when we did *Sweeney Todd.* It was 112 dimmers. It hasn't been that few for a long time: four racks of 32 used to be big—we were still at 96 dimmers for the musicals for a long time. But now we're up to, you know, 800 to 900 dimmers, 1,200 to 1,300 lights, plus peripherals for days, and now I have one electrician.

Where I used to have three electricians to deal with 350 lights, I now have one electrician to deal with so much that he gets buried. And main-

tenance becomes big issues here. Or getting them to hire another contract man or letting the union permit another man to show up, to help
maintain all this stuff. So electricians have a tendency to get buried now.

JANE REISMAN: Neil [Jampolis] and I had just done *Black and Blue*, and
then I was doing a production for one of those off-off-Broadway companies, Willow Cabin, on Forty-second Street. No, it wasn't Forty-
second Street, it hadn't moved there yet, but it was a little tiny room
somewhere—InterArts. I could only have twenty-five units, and I
remember getting such a thrill out of the fact that while I was doing
Black and Blue on Broadway I was running over to this other theatre and
doing this show with twenty instruments, which I said was probably the
best work I'd ever done in my life, and with the most integrity—every
light counted. And I found that much more rewarding than having the
fifty mechanized lights up there in the air on *Black and Blue*.

RICHARD WINKLER: It's amazing how the computer board revolution-
ized the design process. Or, the lack of design process today.

LE: *Can you elaborate on that—the lack of design process—what do you
mean?*

WINKLER: Well, I think there are a whole lot of designers who don't do
enough homework. They put a bunch of stuff in the air with a whole lot
of different variables, color scrollers with the same colors from one show
to the next show, to the next show. Moving lights with the same capabilities, color-wise, from one show to the next show to the next show. And
they then make their choices in the theatre—which is not really designing as far as I'm concerned, because the process of design is all about having conversations and creating a conceptual look. An intellectual conceptual look. Then being able to take that intellectual conceptual look
and translating that in your head from the look of what you want to
angle, color, and design. And then drawing that. And I think that the
modern technology has allowed a lot of people not to do that, and not to
do their homework, but to wait until they get into the theatre.

PARICHY: I don't remember exactly when this is, but very recently I did
some little show where I was back on a two-scene preset board after . . .
a long time. And it was fairly complicated, and I noticed that I sudden-

ly was extraordinarily impatient . . .with the damn thing. I had kind of lost over the course of . . . since 1980 at least . . . the thought process about those things, so I felt really impatient about how to run this cue. I said to myself, "What the hell, what's the problem here?" So, its kind of subtle. I definitely think about cuing completely differently; there's something almost fearless about it now, and also I think in part you don't have to plan as much. One of the things I hate actually about having so many dimmers often is, if you're not careful you indulge yourself and you put every light up in the air, and you have 250 channels of control and you don't really need that. You say, "Oh well, let's just throw in something here and something there," and they're not really things you are committed to using in some strong way. When I've done that I end up either not using them or I find that when I try to use them, I didn't really think it out very well. It's so easy, and no one is really forcing me to make the hard choices about what I could have and what I couldn't have. Because there are so many dimmers and so many units, you can indulge in whatever came along on the spur of the moment. Sometimes that was because I wasn't really sure what the hell that particular show was going to turn out to be like, so it's just easier to throw more units and more dimmers up than to think more carefully about the details in advance.

The "homework" a lighting designer needed to do when shows were run manually included thinking about the operability of the cues. Could two electricians on four piano boards with two auxiliary boards actually execute each cue? Considering this as part of the design meant that designers had to have a very clear idea— before they got into the theatre—of what each cue should look like. They also needed to organize their hookup in a way that would facilitate the operation of the cues. Consideration of the light cues and the organization of the hookup are two related areas of lighting design process that have changed significantly because of computer control consoles.

LE TO KEN BILLINGTON: *In a 1995 interview, you said that computer control has been* the *major technological change. It has changed the way designers think about cues; it has led to color scrollers and moving lights. Could you elaborate or be more specific about the way that computer con-*

trol changed the way that you specifically think about cues?

BILLINGTON: When we were on manual control, you had to have your cues created before you designed the show, because you had to worry about operation. For something as simple as a bump cue from red to blue, you couldn't have half the dimmers on one board going up to red and the other half going down to blue. There was just no way to do that. So you have to have one board with all the reds on it and the other board would have the blues, so the guy could stand in between and his left hand would go up while his right hand went down. So design had to be thought out at the drawing board operationally for what the show was to look like. So that meant that if you were bumping from red to blue and you had the green over with the red because that was just where you had it—one circuit of green—the director saw the green and said, "Oh, you know, instead of running from red to blue, let's run from red to green," you couldn't do it, because then you would have had to do major replugging and recircuiting and rewriting of all the cues of the show. So you didn't have that latitude, but you truly had done all your homework because you had to know how the man was going to operate the show before you lit it. What memory control did is, I no longer have to worry about the director saying, "Well, let's try red and green." OK, we can try red and green. "Though I think it might be wrong, let's take a look at it." As opposed to saying, "Well, we'll look at it tomorrow after I replug all the boards." Cues can be refined, where on manual control you really had four readings. You had 7, 5, 3, and full. And by the way, 3 was three-quarters of intensity.

LE: *Because on resistance boards the readings were reversed?*

BILLINGTON: Yes. Because it was 30 percent resistance actually. So you could get up to 60 and you could get to 20 and you could get to 35 but not often, and it probably would be a special that was moving—one thing, one handle. You couldn't bring fourteen handles up to fourteen different locations. You could bring them up to 50 and then he could unlock some and bring the balance up to 30, but you couldn't get all these minute readings that we do nowadays. So you were more general in your areas. If there was someplace where the cyc had to get to 60 and there was a certain circuit on the cyc, you would say to the man, "In cue 5, handle 32 can't get above 60." And he would flag it and it would never go above 60-something. Not that you couldn't do it—but you really had to pick and choose how important is it really to run these lights at 35 percent.

OSTERMANN: Working on a resistance board, zero was full intensity and 10 was out. I think you should put this in the book, because it was all backwards. You would take the lights up to 1 or down to 7 and everything was backwards, because it was measuring the amount of resistance and not the amount of output. And a lot of shows, when I was working back then in the middle '70s, would start on resistance boards and then would change over to autotransformer boards when they got from out of town to New York previews, and all the cues had to be changed. All the numbers had to be reversed. It was really nasty. And the heat . . . I don't know if anyone's ever talked about the heat. I'll never forget that when I was working on *Truckload* in August [1975] as a second assistant to John Gleason while I was still a student at NYU. John told me to take notes down to the guys. There was no room on stage and no room on the fly floor for the boards so they were all down in the basement, and the basement was probably 6 feet 6 inches high. I remember walking down there in the middle of August, and the heat! It was over 100 degrees down there, the guys were all stripped down to their waists, they had their shirts off, they were just completely sweating on the cue sheets, making them almost illegible. I'll never forget that, how hot and uncomfortable and horrible it was. They had fans going, but it didn't matter because any time a dimmer was off, all of the light would be out but the power would still be being sucked up by the board, and it was all being output as heat. That was a huge thing, all that heat coming out of those boards. So it's so much more comfortable now to run the boards. I think the electricians really have it easier now. Thank God. They have it harder because there are more lights to maintain, but they have it easier because they don't have to work in a sweatshop any more. That's a big, big change.

Everything changed . . . when computers came in. When the boards were manual, we had to design all the light cues before the show. And when the light plot was done, the light cues were done—so that they could be run. If we did a two-board show, for example, and there was a cross-fade between day and night, the warm lamps would be on one board and the cool lamps on the other board, so the cross-fade could happen. It would never be combined. And I think in the old days the designs were better because they all had to be conceived to the end—before the load-in. We knew what the lighting was going to be, most of it—I would say 80 percent of it, so that the cues could be run. Once the computer came in, it didn't matter what the hookup was, because every cue was operable.

JAMPOLIS: In 1976 I began working in Ottawa at the National Arts Centre, lighting operas, and they had a Cue Level . . . that was the first time I got to do big productions with a memory board, and it was quite a revelation. One had to fight a different kind of a battle with them, two battles: the battle of through-line, and the battle of taste.

LE: *Can you elaborate on that?*

JAMPOLIS: When a board that's truly a tracking board—that is, unless somebody grabbed a handle and moved it, the light stayed where it was—you tended to arrive at a look at the beginning of a scene, and then modify it as the scene went on, incrementally, because physically that's all you could do. You had to think about what the lighting looked like and how it would evolve over the course of a scene. When it became possible to go from red stage to blue stage to green stage to whatever, I had to resist the temptation. Because it was very easy to say, "Well, I don't have to think that way any more. I can just put up anything I want." Then, both the through-line of the lighting and the taste went out the window, if you gave in. I think it was a real crisis, for a couple of years, in lighting design, as designers got their hands on this stuff and became seduced by the technology, and abandoned the art, at least temporarily. . . . When we had to set up a show on road boards—I was thinking this the other day, when I was teaching—a manually run show like *Sherlock Holmes* which was on five road boards, you had to think of the look that you wanted, and then do the hookup so that the look could be achieved. Because if the guys couldn't grab the handles in the right places, you'd never get the look. You really had to close your eyes and imagine the lighted stage, and then work backward and figure out where all those handles were. It was a very physical thing. It was almost as physical for the designer, working that out—and remember we used to do it on spreadsheets that you would draw out physically like the boards in their arrangements of dimmers, and then think of the cue and look what was involved in pulling those handles, and getting the thing to look that way. And so you would have your blue-stage board, and your clear board, and your warms and your pinks, and . . . things like that. It was a whole different way of thinking, and . . . in a way there was a transition period I spoke of, where lighting wasn't very good from anybody, for a while, and then it got back on track.

PARICHY: I think we've all tended to change the way we approach cuing now. And the factors of "Is this physically possible?" and "How many men/people does it take to run this show?" as the founding premises are not that important. . . . The biggest show I ever did on resistance boards was *Best Little Whorehouse in Texas,* and to do it that way, we had four or five men running the show—which was an extraordinary number. There was a lot of coordination of who does what and how do we get all these dimmers to move in the right tempo at the same time, et cetera. And then within a few years we stopped thinking about all of those things and thought, "How can we make this more elaborate? What else can we do here?" And it doesn't take that much time if you know how to talk to the board and program it.

LE TO RICHARD WINKLER: *Did your own organizational process change when computer technology became available to you in your own work? Specifically, has the organization of your hookups changed?*

WINKLER: Oh, it changed drastically. . . .

LE: *Can you think of any specific ways in which your hookup organization changed?*

WINKLER: It was only about the loads then, in the road board days. The hookups used to be done when you had a 6K dimmer for the cyc, you put the cyc in the 6K dimmers, and you organized everything so that all of the cyc stuff was together. It was only about organizing things so that the loads would work. Now, it's about—to me—about where, in my head, the order of importance of things in terms of the overall design falls. All of my cyc stuff is always still together. But the cyc stuff can be in the middle of the hookup, or two-thirds of the way through the hookup now. Whereas then, it was always in a specific place because that's where the 6K dimmers were. For instance, if I have six different colors on a cyc, and I also have a couple of different templates on the cyc, now I can put the templates next to the cyc within my overall hookup. As opposed to, in the old days, thinking about where the auxiliary boards were plugged in. For instance, all of my specials are always together in my hookups now. My specials would not necessarily be together in the old days because it was only about where you plugged the auxiliary board and what the master was that was controlling it.

OSTERMANN: There was a huge difference right there—the hookup—how the show was laid out changed drastically. Also, in the old days with the road boards, resistance boards and autotransformer boards, the dimmers were bigger. They were either 3K or 6K dimmers on the resistance boards and they had to be loaded to capacity to function properly; the autotransformer boards were either 3.6K or 6K, so that there was less individual control. Most of the design was in groups of four-lamp washes. Once the computer came in, there were a lot more separate channels for a lot more individual control. On the road boards we had auxiliary boards that were either . . . the standard ones were 8-plate 750-watt or 12-plate 500-watt or something like that for specials. But it was mostly groups of light, big washes of light with a couple of specials in between, and I think now with the computers it's almost a dimmer per channel, if you can afford it.

LE: *Do you mean one light per dimmer?*

OSTERMANN: Yes. One lamp per dimmer. Back in the '70s, when I was working on Broadway, the standard size dimmers were 4Ks when we got into computers. Now it's 2.4K, and we're using more dimmers controlling more individual lights. For me the goal is always to have one lamp on a dimmer for total flexibility like it is in Europe. But it's very expensive to rent that many dimmers.

JAMPOLIS: The very first boards I worked with were dimmer-per-circuit and no cross-patching, so that in itself was a nightmare, because there was absolutely no way to make any mnemonic connections like one does now. Now I have all kinds of stratagems. I guess you stick in a way to the way you originally started, with certain [control channel] numbers being your basic areas, and then odd numbers from the left and even numbers from the right, and so on. But now there are other things, like knowing what board you have, so that the numbers for the scrollers are right under the numbers for the units they're attached to [on the monitor screen]. That way you can always see what lights are up and what positions their scrollers are in, and things like that. There are whole other kinds of stratagems that are now necessary. But I tend to cue to a hookup not necessarily wondering how it was going to run, but just so I could remember things without having to look at papers, which I would hope is the very last resort. . . . One wants to look at the stage and call up a dimmer number from memory, based on where it is on the stage you want the light, and which direction you want it coming from. So if I deviate too far from that, or an assistant who's doing work on it deviates too far from that, I haven't a clue as to how to bring up things without riffling through papers, which I don't like.

WARFEL: I didn't change my organizational method, but how a theatre worked changed. You could still put your cyc stuff at the end [of your hookup], which is just a sort of mental organization thing more than a necessity. The reason for that is that you can assign channels, and you plug into an outlet, and now you can assign that outlet to some control channel. So you have the ability to organize it so that it works in your head. To me it's always been a matter of how it works in your head: What number to think of if you don't have your magic sheet lying in front of you, or if you want to take the quickest route from magic sheet dependence to knowing your numbers in your head, which we all do as we go along. And, all right, let your habits of a lifetime of how you organize a hookup continue to be, because there's no reason to change them.

PARICHY: In the early days [of computer use], I was still thinking, to some extent, "How can this be run?" I had had a lot of practice at Circle Rep with two-scene presets—24, 48, 36 channels, and how can one person run these cues and make them look good. It was always a big, big factor. I still know there are certain ways I tend to arrange my hookups and designs that I learned on resistance boards. And think about that, the kind of groups that we had to do in those days. I've gradually dropped it, but I still have a tendency to think of systems of lights and the kinds of groups that I learned to use on resistance boards, rather than break them down into individually controlled units or anything. And I don't really like most of the time to make too much control. It just gets out of hand often; on the big show you end up finding there's fifteen channels you never used because they just got lost. There were too many numbers to remember, that kind of thing. . . . We had to, in the old days, on the preset boards and the resistance boards, think about, "How can I make all these things happen on eighteen or twenty-four dimmers?" So I tended to group lights in different ways, ways that I wouldn't do any more. Now I break down washes and sidelight into, not really "zones," but I may break the zones up into two or three pieces, whereas in those days I would automatically keep the zones the zones. And sometimes you would have to put in-one, in-two, and in-three all together because that's the only way you could have it, with the limited dimmers and control possibilities. And it took a long time, for me anyway, before I began to modify my practice and adapt to the possibilities.

The biggest change that I remember is the enormous speeding up of the cuing process. One of the main things I remember on the old boards was that if something went wrong, if you had to back up, you could spend half an hour restoring to five cues back, and getting it right. Whereas suddenly, with computers, about all you had to do was press a button and you could move back to that old cue and you didn't have to worry about it. You had the levels there; you didn't have to figure out what they actually were at that point. That was the biggest change and the most obvious one that I recall. It was only, as I said, several years later that the subtler possibilities began to be clear to me. And now one of those things had to do with the fact that I was still doing a lot of little shows, and it was several years before the majority of the shows were being run on some version of a memory board.

DANA: I don't think that my hookups have changed at all. The only thing that's changed in my hookups now is that instead of listing channel 1 as four lamps, channel 1 is now either one or two lamps. That's the only difference. I do not subscribe to the theory that because you're on computers you can put a channel anywhere [in a hookup]. You must group channels in order to make things work properly. How do you keep your mind straight about it? If you've got area 1 on channel 1, and area 2 on channel 23, and area 4 on channel 16, how do you keep track of that? It's a cluttered mind that comes up with that kind of organization. I'm not saying that there aren't places where things get totally out of sequence and weird, particularly on a show that goes squirrelly on you one way or another. And all of a sudden things end up with different purposes and so on. But at least you should be starting by some kind of grouping in terms of function. Just as it used to be easier to grab hold of a stick and run up ten dimmers on a two-scene preset (if the ten dimmers were adjacent to each other, because you knew that the back light would all work together), it's the same thing on a computer: 1 through 10 is easier to say and fewer keystrokes than anything else. Now, if you didn't group all that stuff, when you look at the screen, how do you know what's up? So I think there needs to be some kind of organization along those lines. Now, the one thing that may have changed . . . well, even then it hasn't changed, for me at least. One through 10 are my areas, and then I'm going to start the next block of, say, high sidelight or something like that at 21, and it'll go from 21 to wherever it ends, and the next, say that's high sidelight in-1, and then high sidelight in-2 is going to start at, say, 41, or whatever. All right, I'm going to start with 1 all the time. Because 1 is the first of everything and, working left to right, you can get a block. And it's easier to look at the screen and see that block, that group. And then I will dump in the spaces that are left in between. If, for instance, I've used 1 to 15 for area light and I have 16 through 20 open, that's where I'll put specials. . . . I'll dump specials into those holes. . . . But I don't think that my hookup has changed . . . in any significant way. I still put my cyc lights at the back end, because cyc lights usually get placed someplace and left alone for a long period of time, so I put it on a high screen so I don't have to look at it all the time. I put everything together, you know . . . I don't think that there's really been any significant change to what it is I do. Except that, as I say, there's more of it.

Americans used to use large dimmers and group a lot of things, based on road boards and the necessity to put four lamps on a dimmer to make it work. The Brits tended to use a dimmer per circuit—put a light on each circuit. They had larger circuits and larger boards, two-scene presets or five-scene presets, because they had more operators to run the show. We had fewer operators, so we ganged things on smaller control. The computer now gave us the chance to keep our manpower either the same or less than it had been before, and as a result we started moving more and more quickly towards having a dimmer per circuit and being able to break up our stuff into smaller and smaller pieces. So that now we tend to handle a mosaic of smaller and smaller tiles than ever before, and as a result we're going for smaller and smaller detail, and we're building up a picture by being able to group these tiles of the mosaic in different ways. The same thing started to occur there. It used to be a standard that a play by Shakespeare is eighty cues. Now Shakespeare is two hundred cues, because you can do more. Because you can get the subtlety and have a moment come up, and it would be OK. You don't have to worry any more about leveling the dimmers. You don't have to worry so much about how many presets can you set, and how many preset operators there are, and all of that kind of stuff. So now one man or woman has a great deal more control over the entire panoply. It makes cuing sessions longer, but results are infinitely more subtle.

LE: *Does it make the cuing sessions longer because people are writing more cues?*

DANA: Writing more cues, and there is more detail. It's very difficult to do even a straight play where you're not looking at a couple of cues per page [of text]. I don't tend to work that way, because I don't subscribe to the theory that seems to be prevalent that if the eye is left alone for a period of time that it will grow tired and weary and won't look at the stage. I think it actually gives a chance to rest. And I also think that when the people walk around, they change the stage picture so that the eye is not looking at the same thing all the time.

By the early 1990s, movement on stage was no longer the result solely of actors moving about the stage—lights were moving, or "wiggling," as well. After control protocols were standardized in the 1980s, automated lights became accessible to theatrical designers and had an impact on lighting design parallel to that of the first computer control consoles. The designer's toolbox could now include not only four hundred lights in four hundred individual control channels, but some (or all) of those lights could change color, focus position, even light quality. As did computer control, automation has altered the process and product of theatrical lighting.

REISMAN: I've been watching people's lighting. Now that you can turn a gobo any way you want, there seems to be a lack of . . . composition. I seem to find a lot of gobos used not when you have to do it for a reason, but just because it doesn't matter, from any point source to the stage. And the question of where is this light coming from . . . sometimes it disturbs me to watch lighting in which where the light is coming from is no longer an issue—I'm talking about composition. When you can go anywhere you want it's not the light in the air any more. So, put some smoke in the air and then they can see what's going on. But that point of where the light's coming from is fascinating to me at this point. I think lighting composition has changed a lot.

LE: *Do you think part of that has to do with less realism in the theatre, though?*

REISMAN: Perhaps. But then, those are design choices, you know. It may have something to do with that. But then why have a window gobo coming through something that you say is a window if it's coming from somewhere else? Yes, it's perhaps less that, but I think it's an interesting change I've just been seeing recently, very recently.

DAVIS: The problem today, with all the moving lights and all the dimmers, no one has to think up anything before they go in the theatre. You just hang enough stuff, and have enough scrollers, and have enough moving lights, you can always make the concept up in the theatre. Which I think is a sort of nasty thing.

DANA: There's a serious problem now with moving lights. . . . I'll mention a particular show, though there are several of them. Everybody I know who saw a particular Broadway show from the ground floor thought that the lighting was brilliant. Everybody I know who saw it from the balcony thought it sucked. The reason why is that from the balcony you were aware that the stage was filled with lights having Tourette's syndrome in extremis. Because you place a moving light some place, and record it, then you move on to the next thing, and there's some minor adjustment down the line, and some parameter of the moving light is off by one point. Or you say, "Let's go back to cue 5," because that's what we're restoring. So you go back to cue 5 and you restore, but cue 5 now has one parameter off by two tenths of a point from where you were in cue 11, and you're trying to record cue 11 as cue 12. So now when you go to 11, everything should be tracking through to cue 12. But it isn't. Everything twitches to its false location. It twitches in color, it twitches in movement, it twitches in size, it twitches in . . . how much diffusion is in.

I was watching a Broadway show for the Tony awards, and I'm sitting in the fourth row, which is a great place to watch the lighting from [laughter]. And . . . there's this wonderful scene . . . very nicely lit with a moving light that's gone to a place with a table downstage left. And it's there and it's nice and it's clean. And the light moves, not that light but the other lights on the stage move in order to move your focus over to downstage right, where a scene is going on. And your eye follows the movement of that light, it goes over to the other side, and then out of the corner of your eye you see the first light twitch. Did it close or open? I think it opened, almost 9 inches. We cannot have a stage filled with Tourette's syndrome.

REISMAN: There's a lot of lighting that's for af-fect, or effect only. . . . But there's still wonderful designers out there doing beautiful work . . . a lot of beautiful, beautiful work around right now. So it's very exciting.

LE TO KEN BILLINGTON: *Do you think that because you've really embraced all these new technologies—scrollers and moving lights—your design process in the studio changed as well? Has your preproduction process changed knowing that you have all this stuff available to you?*

BILLINGTON: Yes, absolutely. It changed in that for a musical—where your backlight would be border lights, PAR56 or PAR64 border lights—you would get three colors; any three colors you would want, but that would be your backlight. Now if you had two pipes you could maybe have six colors, but that never happened. I always think you always need the blue, so you're going to have the blue and then you need the warm because there's going to be . . . it just makes sense. Now this is just being very general, but that left you the third color. So what does this show need that you can do with the third color? Well, we go to a nightclub twice—shall we do magenta? Well, then we have the underwater scene, maybe we need green. So you had to follow through on what was that third color that's going to make it look good. With the color scroller, I always have my blue and then I have the color scroller, so I know I have my warm and I have my blue—the green for the underwater and my magenta for the nightclub. And it's just made that process a little less angst-driven and maybe made the scene look better. Because we go to the nightclub three times and we only go underwater once, so what's more important?

So that's where that all developed from. I think that part [having more ability to have multiple color choices] made life a lot easier. And, it just makes the show look better. I still think you need to think about what color the green is and what color the magenta is. Of course, now with the color-fader things you don't even have to think about that. You can pick any magenta you want.

Digital developments changed not only the functions and aesthetics of theatrical lighting, but altered the role of the lighting designer's support personnel as well. When shows were run on resistance dimmers, or early electronic consoles with manual or analog electronic controllers, the assistant lighting designer had broad but fairly uniformly proscribed duties. These included drafting and paperwork preparation in the preproduction phase, keeping records of the focus of the lights, preparation of operator cue sheets, and maintenance of a tracking paper archive of the show's cues throughout the technical rehearsal process. Even when computers were used that could "remember" cues, the assistant lighting designer (ALD) sat next to the lighting designer and wrote down channel levels in each cue—he or she functioned as a real-time human printer. In fact, the ability to use peripheral printers was a technological advance that did not happen until the early 1980s. The computer control consoles of the 1970s and 1980s were also notoriously unstable. If the ALD did not accurately record each cue on paper, or at least a method of restoring the cue from previous cues, then if the computer console failed, entire shows could be lost and have to be reprogrammed—in a way redesigned—from the beginning.

I asked Richard Winkler if he had to develop a new way of keeping track of cues when *A Chorus Line* moved on to the LS-8 memory console.

WINKLER: We did it the way we had always done it.

LE: *The way you would have kept track of things on resistance dimmers?*

WINKLER: Yes. Because we weren't sophisticated enough then.

The LS-8, like most computer control consoles of that time, did not have a remote monitor on the lighting designer's table front-of-house. If there was a monitor at all, there was just the one screen at the operator's console. Designers relied on their assistants to keep a running track of the light cues because that would be their primary access to the cue information during technical rehearsals.

As computer systems became more stable and printers much faster and more available than in the early days, the role of the assistant lighting designer has evolved.

DANA: We all have those stories, where we've overwritten the show the wrong way; all of that kind of stuff has occurred at one time or another. We've all played those games. And every once in a while you have to get brought up short and re-recognize the fact that you're going to make mistakes and that you should disk out continually. There are people like Billington who still use the track sheet.[2] One of the things that has happened is that I don't, because I depend upon that board. I do not track shows; I think it's a waste of my assistant's time to track a show.

LE: *I still use track sheets myself. I often work with less-experienced operators and it's critical that there be track sheets because even now, they'll just accidentally hit the wrong button, and they'll load the show from yesterday*

---

2. A "track sheet" is a form, usually laid out to look similar to the computer's stage monitor for channel readings, on which the ALD keeps the cue record, usually one cue per page, along with placement of the cue in the script and the cue's function.

instead of recording the show from today, and it's gone. Have you lost information because there is no running record?

<u>DANA:</u> Yes, I have.

<u>LE:</u> *But you don't feel the trade-off is worth it to have an assistant keep a running track?*

<u>DANA:</u> No . . . I do not use an assistant. The way I function with an assistant is that I . . . have a team, and my name is on the title page because I head the team. My name is there because I decide to accept or reject ideas that come from anywhere; from myself, from my assistant, from my board operator, from the director—who the hell cares, right? But I decide to use the ideas, and that's why my name's on the title page to take the credit or the blame for having done that. And therefore I want my assistant to be a contributing member of what goes on. So my assistant has a primary responsibility for keeping the paper up. But I help the assistant keep the paper up, and I want the assistant to use their eyes and see things. I want an assistant who sees something and says to me, "Did you want to use that? Or did you want to leave that one over there?" Or I say, "How the hell am I going to light them up there?" (as I said last night). "How about 173?" my assistant can say. I want somebody who is a partner. I figure, the more eyes we have working on this, the more problems we're going to catch. If they see something move out of the corner of their eye that distracts them, that's good. Because they bring it to my attention. It distracted them, but it shouldn't distract them. And I just missed it because I'm focusing on something else. And you can develop a tunnel vision of one form or another. It's hard to look back and see the whole picture, so I want someone who looks at the rest of the picture and sees what goes on, a different sensibility to be brought to it. It seems to me that there is no reason to assist, if in fact you're not allowed to contribute.

<u>LE:</u> *Right, exactly. I always found that my most enjoyable assisting experiences were those in which the designer treated me as a design associate rather than merely an archival secretary.*

<u>DANA:</u> It can be a total waste of everybody's time to assist a designer who wants to feel that the job is top-down and ideas from the bottom (i.e.,

the assistant) are not relevant. I recommend to my students that they be very careful if they assist, because they can learn style, but if you find a designer who's like that, recognize what the trade-off is. Put the time in to get the experience and the credit and a couple of other things, but move up. Find the designers who want you to be part of the team.

LE TO NEIL PETER JAMPOLIS: *Do you still have assistants keep track sheets manually, keeping a running track while you are doing a show?*

JAMPOLIS: No.

LE: *When did you stop doing that?*

JAMPOLIS: Five or six years ago—maybe more. When the boards became reliable. When boards got hard drives in them, so that almost any place in the proceedings when there was a break, you could say, "Make it this, go record that, or keep it." And when the printout wasn't a dot-matrix printer with fanfold paper that would go on through the lunch hour and on for the next three hours . . . all of those things. When you could take the disk and put it in your computer and look at it in your off-line editor to do your tracking. All of those things helped. And now what I find is that my assistants tend, rather than tracking, to do cue descriptions on the fly.

LE: *What do you mean by that?*

JAMPOLIS: That they will sit there with their laptops. And as I'm working, they are watching the stage and describing what the cue is and where it goes, so that there's a kind of running cue list going that's descriptive rather than numerical. And it's very helpful for stage management, of course. It's easier to do then than to go back after the show is written. And I admire their skill. I certainly couldn't have done it when I was an assistant.

Mitch Dana related the complications of using moving lights to the responsibility of the assistant lighting designer.

DANA: Where is that responsibility for a stage filled with twitching lights? One of those responsibilities is the assistant who was not tracking. And the assistant did not watch what was going on. And the assistant did not contribute. Now, it may have been that that particular assistant was prohibited from making comments of that nature. And as a result they're not fed in, and we get this problem. And of course on Broadway now, the boards aren't even where anybody can see anything, so the board operator can't even see if the light is twitching. And in that particular place, I happen to know, if the board operator had called down and said, "That light just twitched," he would have been told to shut up.

LE: *Interesting . . . and one of the reasons I stopped assisting.*

When I did stop assisting, it was to begin a career teaching lighting design and designing for not-for-profit professional theatres. Many of the people I interviewed have likewise combined a teaching career with a professional design career. I asked them to share their views on the ways that changing technologies have altered their teaching methodologies.

LE TO BILL WARFEL: *Did you change your teaching patterns or methodology at all because suddenly there was new, flexible technology?*

WARFEL: No. I didn't. I most certainly did not . . . because I'm a minimalist kind of designer. I keep things very simple. I was trained by Stanley McCandless in the 1950s. And those were impoverished times compared to the kind of money that even modestly endowed theatre programs have available to them now. We had very, very little money. And McCandless, of course, had invented a method of lighting the stage, as he called it,[3] and it was extremely simple. And even though I didn't continue to design shows according to those particular procedures, I was constantly cognizant of [using] a minimum number of lights. My designing and my teaching have always gone the way of "if you're going to accomplish something, think of the simplest way to accomplish it first." Then, if you want to expand and add two more lights because it makes it better, and as more ideas happen you want to

---

3. McCandless' book, *A Method of Lighting the Stage,* 4th ed. (New York: Theatre Arts Books, 1958), was first published in 1932. It was the first book to codify twentieth-century stage lighting techniques.

put those on . . . but think of the simplest approach, the basic approach to the show. Memory boards didn't change that. Of course, memory boards made some difference in that at some point along in there—I don't remember when it was—I stopped teaching people how to design according to loading a resistance dimmer. Because the union exam[4] was no longer "you live or die depending on the fact you know about piano boards." But, it was not a change in how a show should be lighted; it was a change in what you have available now to realize it.

DANA: I believe that if you're teaching technology, you're teaching design, you're teaching how to use your eye, how to think about the script and about the subtext and about what the play is about, and what it is you're trying to communicate. But, as with everything of course, the technology is the means to the end, and I at least partially resent the amount of technology and the desire of most of the students to get themselves involved in the technology to the exclusion of the art. And then they all seem to think that they can sit down with these [memory control] boards without having to spend any time working on them. They don't know how they work, they're only using a portion of their abilities, they're not asking questions . . . they're not even looking at them as something to be conquered and made into a tool. It's as if they were painters, and they wanted to paint, but they didn't want to have any knowledge about how to clean brushes or buy brushes or which brush to use. It's very frustrating. And I don't know how one goes about teaching the technology really well, I mean at least in terms of the boards. Because running a board—I mean, you can sit down there and you can teach them and you can tell them all the various bells and whistles and how it works. But in reality, until they see it happen and they are able to perceive the difference between running a cue this way and running a cue that way . . . it's of no value. And if they don't perceive that difference, which is a design difference, then the technology is kind

---

4. Warfel refers here to the entrance exam to join United Scenic Artists Local 829 IATSE (then IBPAT), the union of professional lighting designers, set designers, costume designers, and scenic artists.

5. Most contemporary control consoles enable the designer to split a cue into different parts and operate each part at an individualized rate. Doing so often allows for more fluidity of movement of light than would multiple cues, but not all consoles are able to record part cues in an efficient manner.

of useless, isn't it?

For example, is it better to do parts,[5] or is it better to do multiple cues? What are the advantages and disadvantages of each? I think that you can teach that all intellectually, but the problem in the running of boards is it really never comes to fruition, it never becomes internalized until they're on stage with a show under circumstances where they have to do something, and they don't know how to do it. Or we're at a tech, and there are a lot of people standing around; it's not the best time to sit down and show them [the student lighting designer] the relative advantages between six part cues and six individual cues on auto follows. So I'm not quite sure how to go about dealing with a lot of that stuff; the time that's necessary to deal with it. Also, running board, you don't really become good at running a board until you sit in the seat, and you get you or me saying, as we do, "Let me have this channel at this level, this at that, that at that, this at that, record, track, next. Over to page—OK, change the time on that"—that kind of pressure, you can't do that in a classroom. It never exists.

LE: *It certainly seems to me that production is the best place to teach and learn those skills.*

DANA: From my standpoint, I think that set designers and costume designers can do a great deal of work in the classroom and in the homework projects. Because so much of it can be accomplished and realized through the model and the sketch and so on, ground plans and so on, so that you have a really good idea of what it is that's going to end up on stage. Certainly maybe 40 or 50 percent of it can be done that way. But with lighting design, I don't know, that light plot represents maybe 10 or 15 percent of what ends up happening. The rest of it has to happen with real people . . .

LE: *I've actually stopped having my students do too many light plots, because it becomes just this rote exercise and they're not getting much out of it, and you're right, it's only 10 percent of the design.*

DANA: In fact, my first-year class is all about reading scripts, functions and quality of lighting . . . because I think that you can never go over enough looking at the functions and qualities and looking at what happens when you have an attached shadow or a not-attached shadow, what happens when you light with shin busters, and how do you make people appear to float, and how do you bring out texture, and how do you tone, and how do you separate, and how do you create focus. . . . Those are all intellectual concepts, and they're all design concepts, and they're all about what it's about if I want to turn out designers, not technicians. So, what I'm after is to train their eye and to train their interpretive abilities, their ability to see. We don't reveal tricks; when you're walking around, you say, "Ah, look at that shadow. See that? Where's that coming from? Look, see how that room does that? Where's that texture coming from?" Just to get people to open their eyes and start seeing things! Because their research lab is all around them.

But they don't see it, you know. They keep thinking they have to go to the light lab in order to figure this stuff out. But that's only how to recreate it. In the first place, you have to know what it is you're trying to create. So, that's what my first year's all about, is basically that. Plus, I do a certain amount of Kelvin temperature and all that, and exactly how to figure out what units you're going to use, and distance and multiplying factors and so on, so you have the technical tools, but that's all that really is. All the rest is application.

"Application" is key. How are technological tools "applied" in the service of the art of theatre? There has been so much new development in the twenty-year period discussed here that the function of stage lighting has been fundamentally altered. And technological advances have enabled stage lighting techniques to be applied in retail lighting, restaurants, and even people's homes.

At the time of this writing, just following the 2001 Tony awards, the top award winners were shows based on films: *The Producers* and *The Full Monty.* It is the technology, both lighting and scenic, that has enabled live theatre performance to become so fluid, so cinematic. The chicken-and-egg question posed earlier cannot be answered. However, the omelette that results is a rich, exciting, new form of theatrical production.

Interview Subject
Capsule Biographies

KEN BILLINGTON has designed over seventy shows on Broadway, winning the 1997 Tony award for the revival of *Chicago*. Since the 1970s he has been the lighting designer for Radio City Music Hall's *Christmas Spectacular*. Also in the 1970s, he designed such Broadway hits as *On the Twentieth Century* (which used resistance dimmers) and *Side by Side by Sondheim* (which used an early memory-based console). Interview date: October 1999.

ALLEN BRANTON is a designer of lighting for live concert events and television. He was one of the first designers to use Vari-Lites who was not also an employee of the manufacturer. Major projects with early Vari-Lites included concert tours by David Bowie, Diana Ross, Ozzie Osbourne, and Whitney Houston. Interview date: May 30, 1997.

DAVE CUNNINGHAM has been developing products for the lighting industry since the late 1960s when he worked for George Van Buren, developer of one of the first computer control consoles. He later worked for Strand, where he developed the CD80 dimmer, and then formed his own company, Entertec. With Entertec, he developed ENR dimmers for Kliegl and then went on, with partner Greg Esakoff, to develop the

Source 4 fixture for Electronic Theatre Controls. Interview date: August 31, 2000.

F. MITCHELL DANA is a lighting designer for regional theatre, Broadway, and opera. He also teaches lighting design at Rutgers University. He designed *Joseph and the Amazing Technicolor Dreamcoat* in 1975. Interview date: June 25, 1997.

JEFF DAVIS is a lighting designer working throughout regional theatre as well as television. He served in the 1990s as resident lighting designer for New York City Opera. Interview date: June 13, 1997.

BILL FLORAC was an engineer with Lighting Methods, Inc. (LMI), when he was instrumental in developing the USITT DMX512 standard control protocol for console-to-dimmer communication. He is currently in the MIS department at Electronic Theatre Controls. Interview date: August 6, 1998.

FRED FOSTER is founder and president of Electronic Theatre Controls, a leading manufacturer of dimming, control, and lighting equipment. Interview date: January 8, 1998.

MITCH HEFTER is currently an engineer with Entertainment Technology as well as engineering commissioner of USITT. He was commissioner in 1986 when USITT adopted the DMX512 standard. At that time he was an engineer with Strand Lighting. Interview date: August 19, 1998.

NEIL PETER JAMPOLIS has designed both scenery and lighting extensively throughout the 1970s, 1980s, and 1990s. In 1992 he made his directorial debut with the Seattle Opera. He won the Tony award for lighting in 1975 for *Sherlock Holmes* and is on the faculty of UCLA. Interview date: June 19, 1997.

NATASHA KATZ has amassed an impressive list of Broadway credentials since 1988. She has designed such megamusicals as *Beauty and the Beast*, *Aida* (for which she won the 2000 Tony award for lighting), and *Suessical*. She also designed the Las Vegas extravaganza *EFX*, the subject of our interview. Interview date: June 19, 1997.

TOM LITTRELL is marketing manager for Vari-Lite. He was the first operator/engineer for these moving fixtures when they went out on tour in 1981 with the band *Genesis*. Interview date: May 22, 1997.

CURT OSTERMANN is currently the lighting director of the *Maury Pauvich Show* and other live television events as well as being on the faculty at NYU Tisch School of the Arts. He has designed extensively for regional theatre and in the late 1970s was assistant lighting designer (to Tharon Musser) on numerous touring productions of *A Chorus Line*. Interview date: June 12, 1997.

DENNIS PARICHY has designed over four hundred productions, many of them during the period under discussion. Included in these is the original Broadway production of *Best Little Whorehouse in Texas*, one of the last shows on Broadway to use resistance dimmers (road boards). Interview date: June 2, 1997.

GORDON PEARLMAN is president of Entertainment Technology, developer of the IPS dimming system and the "Horizon" lighting control system. Early in his career, he developed the LS-8, the first computer control console used on Broadway. Interview date: July 3, 1997.

JANE REISMAN has designed lighting throughout the United States and Europe. She garnered a Tony nomination for lighting design for *Black and Blue*. Interview date: June 23, 1997.

BRAD RODRIGUEZ was a software engineer for Strand during the mid 1980s when the move toward standardization resulted in the adoption of both the digital protocol DMX512 and the analog protocol AMX192 that he authored. Rodriguez left lighting to pursue a career developing imbedded microchips for other industries. Interview date: August 11, 1998.

STEVE TERRY was, for most of the period under discussion, the executive vice president of Production Arts Lighting in New York. An industry leader, he was instrumental in the movement toward standardized control protocols. Early in his career, he was a substitute electrician on *A Chorus Line* as well as the man responsible for keeping the original console working. Interview date: April 30, 1996.

WILLIAM WARFEL is principal of Warfel Schrager Architectural Lighting, LLC. He taught lighting design at Yale School of Drama for twenty-six years and is the author of *The Handbook of Stage Lighting Graphics*. Warfel's Broadway credits include *The Blood Knot* and *The Father*. Coincidentally, his current business partner, Sara Schrager, ran the two-scene preset console on *A Chorus Line* when it was running off-Broadway at the Public Theatre in 1975. Interview date: June 4, 1997.

MARC B. WEISS has designed lighting for more than 250 productions, including *Deathtrap* in 1978, *Cat on a Hot Tin Roof*, and *Design for Living*. Interview date: June 9, 1997.

RICHARD WINKLER designs extensively for opera, Broadway, and regional theatres. Our interview centered around his experience as Tharon Musser's assistant on the original production of *A Chorus Line*. Interview date: June 6, 1997.